12-5-78

BIRDS OF MAN'S WORLD

BIRDS OF MAN'S WORLD

DEREK GOODWIN

LINE ILLUSTRATIONS BY

ROBIN PRYTHERCH

BRITISH MUSEUM (NATURAL HISTORY)

CORNELL UNIVERSITY PRESS

ITHACA AND LONDON

First published 1978 by Cornell University Press.

International Standard Book Number (cloth) 0–8014–1167–X
Library of Congress Catalog Card Number 77–74922

Printed in Great Britain by Butler & Tanner Ltd, Frome and London

CONTENTS

FOREWORD

Many books have been written about birds and man, but apparently none has been devoted, as this book is, to the ways in which birds have adjusted themselves to a world dominated by man. And yet as man increases and his influence becomes ever more pervasive, the qualities that enable a bird to survive in man's world will become more important; and it will be important for ornithologists to understand them if we are to retain a rich bird fauna.

Derek Goodwin is especially well qualified to write on this topic. Thirty years' service on the staff of the Bird Section of the British Museum (Natural History) have given him an exceptionally wide knowledge of the birds of the world, as far as that knowledge can be acquired from dead specimens and from literature. Wide reading and a retentive memory enable him to produce apt quotations illustrating the past relationship of birds and man. But what uniquely qualifies him is his experience of birds 'in the field' – though the jargon in this case is a little misleading, since it must also be taken to mean 'in the town'. Acute powers of observation, a deep sympathy with birds, and a lifetime of watching them have given him an unrivalled first-hand knowledge of the birds of many countries and especially of the ways in which they interact with man. It will be obvious to the reader that he misses no opportunity of observing birds, and that observations made in what the conventional birdwatcher might think the most unpromising circumstances are put to as good use as any. A delay at a railway station or a walk down a town street yields material that, with careful observation and critical interpretation, is of deeper interest than any rarity glimpsed at a sewage farm.

This is, then, not just another popular bird book. It certainly deserves to be popular, but at the same time it contains original observations that will add to the pleasure and widen the understanding of any ornithologist, even the most learned.

D. W. SNOW

INTRODUCTION

Most people who take pleasure in wild birds are distressed at the number of species that have recently become extinct, and concerned at the still greater number that are scarce or decreasing. This is as it should be because, of bird species that have become extinct within historic times, man is in many cases known, and in the others suspected, to have been directly or indirectly responsible for their extermination. Similarly, with many of the species that are scarce or decreasing, the reason for their scarcity or decline is because they have been persecuted by man or been unable to cope with the changes in their environment brought about by him.

Many birds have, however, managed to thrive alongside man, often because of, rather than in spite of the changes he has brought about. Such species are often ignored, especially if they are seen daily in numbers around our dwellings, but they are not less worthy of our interest and admiration than are rarer and less successful birds. Nor are they, viewed objectively, less aesthetically exciting. The Wood Pigeon is as beautiful as the Avocet, the Magpie as splendid as the Chough.

Familiarity does not always breed contempt but too often it does so. We tend to take for granted the common birds of field and town, assuming that they, like the poor, are always with us. Whereas, however, we can find no reason to dare to hope that one day there will be no poor people, we may justifiably fear that at some future date there *might* be no more common wild birds. Already many of them depend for their success partly on our charity or tolerance; as more

1

refined and selective methods of destroying creatures officially designated as 'pests' become possible an increasing number of species will do so. True, the pest of yesterday, if our efforts against it have succeeded, becomes the protected and highly romanticised rarity of today. It may, however, then be too late, as it was with the Passenger Pigeon.

I have here dealt mainly with species that are successful at living in man's world, and discussed some of the aspects of their inter-relationship with man. In most cases their ability to thrive at close quarters with him in environments which he has created or greatly modified for his own purposes is clearly due to their natural adaptations to their *original* environment.

For the birds of man's world fortune is liable to fluctuate even more rapidly and unpredictably than for those creatures living in more natural situations. (For convenience I here use the term 'natural' in the sense of 'unaffected by man'.) For example, in the Middle Ages the Kite was an abundant and ever-present scavenger in London and the bane of poultry-keepers in almost every village. Now only a relict population of British Kites persists in Wales. The first Collared Dove to reach Britain did so in 1952. Now it is a common suburban and village bird from the Scillies to the Shetlands. Inevitably, therefore, any book dealing with such a subject is bound to be out of date in some particulars by the time it is published.

A work of this size obviously cannot cover the subject fully. I have, therefore, had to be selective, and I must admit to having been heavily biased towards those species, and aspects of their behaviour, which I am fortunate enough to have been able to observe myself. I hope, however, that all who are interested in the birds around them, either when at home or when in distant lands, will find something here to interest them.

CHAPTER ONE

MAN AND THE ENVIRONMENT

One of the most obvious differences between man and birds is that birds have to adapt themselves to fit their environment whereas man deliberately alters his environment to make it fit him. This is, of course, a generalisation; the difference, as with most differences between man and other animals, is not absolute. Birds do make some alterations to their environment that serve to make it more suitable for them; for example the woodpeckers that chisel and hammer out holes in which to nest.

Sometimes the long-term effects of a bird's actions may be considerable. Jays and Nutcrackers, by their burying, respectively, acorns and cedar nuts for future use, cause the spread of oaks and cedar-pines (*Pinus cembra*). A storm-foundered fruit dove starves to death on some tree-less coral islet, but it first excretes the undigested fruit stones from its last meal, and as a result, hundreds of years later, the next hurricane-blown member of its species that lands there finds food and shelter. No other creature, however, alters large areas of land so quickly and to so great an extent as does man.

Everyone sees many examples of man-made environmental change. One revisits a place one lived in only a few years before and finds instead of the copse where one used to picnic a suburban housing estate, and that House Sparrows, Starlings and Feral Pigeons have replaced the former Bullfinches, Willow Warblers and Turtle Doves. A reed-fringed lake, where one used to fish and watch Great Crested Grebes, Moorhens and Sedge Warblers, may be filled in by the local council who have created in its place an ornamental garden (so-called), whose lawns and geometrical beds of gaudy geraniums provide good worm-hunting ground for the local Blackbirds but little of interest to the naturalist. Even such apparently small and local changes may, and indeed commonly do, cause considerable alteration in a country's bird life.

The forests fall

From early times man has been a destroyer of forests with axe and fire; to make clearings to grow his crops, to obtain fuel and building wood, to get rid of wolves or human enemies (this is said to have been the reason for the burning of much of the original Scottish forests), or because people accustomed to living in open country often find the presence of even small patches of forest unpleasing. Chinese settlers in Manchuria in the early part of this century, for example, deliberately burned off the forest even on hills and high ridges where they could neither use the land nor harvest the resultant charcoal.

What effect forest destruction has on the forest birds depends, of course, on the particular circumstances: not only on the different types of destruction – such as how quickly the forest is felled or burned, how completely it is destroyed, whether there are other areas nearby and so on – but also on the type of forest, whether tropical rain forest, northern conifer forest, temperate deciduous forest and so on. It is possible, however, to draw a general picture of the sort of things that result, although it must of course be understood that the exact details of what happens will differ in almost every case.

When a large area of forest is completely cleared in a short time, as often happens where modern methods are used, the result is disaster for all the birds living there. They cannot live in the resultant clearing, they must find new homes elsewhere or die. Usually, and this applies particularly to tropical rain forests, each suitable piece of forest will already have as many birds of each species living in it as it can support. Therefore, if the displaced birds go elsewhere into the forest they will compete with others of their kind already there. As a result some may starve, more than usual (in that area) may be caught by predators, or the effects of competition may mean that breeding is less successful than usual. Almost always the end result will be that the total population is reduced, by the death of about the same number of individuals as was displaced from the felled areas. It is not true of most habitats that the birds 'can go somewhere else' if their environment is ruined for them by man, and it is almost never true of birds of primary forest. They might truly say, like Shylock, 'You take my life when you do take the means whereby I live.'

Where small areas of forest are cleared by more primitive, or at least less thoroughly destructive methods some of the birds may actually benefit and their numbers increase. These are the species that like to live or feed in or on the edge of clearings. Such clearings occur in nature through large trees falling, landslides, fires caused by lightning, or where streams or rivers run through the forest. Where man creates fairly small clearings, or large ones with many trees left standing, such species often find much better conditions for themselves or, to put it more precisely, more extensive areas of suitable habitat than they did originally.

Under primitive methods of agriculture, which are still quite widely practised in many places, and particularly in some where the natural vegetation is tropical forest, clearings are often planted with crops for a few years and then abandoned and new ones are cleared. Under such conditions there will always be, within the same locality, some areas planted to crops, some abandoned clearings growing up with weeds and bushes, and others with varying stages of secondary tree growth. Under these conditions birds are often very abundant, more so, at least in terms of individuals, than in the primeval forest. Also species that naturally inhabit open savanna country or scrubland may invade the forest area and populate the clearings or at least those of them at a stage which reproduce, to some extent, their natural savanna habitat.

Field and farmland

Much of the countryside of Britain and most other European countries consists of farmland, largely pasture or arable fields. The same is true of North America and, although perhaps to a lesser extent, of many other parts of the world. Usually this farmland is rich in bird life unless too free use has been made of herbicides and insecticides, or unless every little bit of cover and waste land has been removed. Even such modern and 'progressive' types of farmland may support, much to the farmer's annoyance, a very large temporary bird population at harvest time or shortly before it, but this usually consists of few species and these usually breed in woods, reedbeds or other cover away from the fields they plunder.

If we consider a few of the common birds of fields and farmlands we soon realise what alterations in the numbers of some birds must have taken place throughout vast areas where man now farms and which were once primeval forest or boggy marshland. Perhaps the most characteristic bird of British fields is the Skylark. It is naturally a bird of open country, and it probably occurred here and there on bare uplands and in the few other tree-less areas; but man felled the forest and, all unwittingly, provided it with a place to live. Until then it must have been absent from most of Britain and many parts of Europe and Asia where it is now widespread.

Much the same is true of the Crested Lark which does not live in Britain but is even more common in many parts of Europe than the Skylark. The Crested Lark is, or rather was, primarily a bird of arid steppe and semi-desert country, and it is still very common in such places. It has, however, also taken advantage of man's destruction of forests. It naturally frequents rather more arid cultivated areas than the Skylark and may often now be found also in any bits of open 'artificial semi-desert' such as are often provided by railway sidings and their surroundings, by the waste ground adjacent to barracks and other institutions, and near roadways and similar places.

In England the Shorelark or Horned Lark is known as a winter visitor to the bleak eastern shores. In Europe and Asia it is everywhere a bird of Arctic tundra, barren mountain plateaux or deserts, and it is replaced by other species of larks in more fertile regions. In America, however, where it is the only true lark – at least it was before the introduction of the Skylark – it used to be found widely in the more arid areas of prairie and steppe desert. Like the Skylark and Crested Lark in the Old World, it has spread into man-made fields. From what I have seen, the Shorelark prefers that these should either be rather arid or have mainly bare soil, leaving lushly-growing pasture fields for other ground-living birds. Even so its range must have been greatly increased by man's destruction of some of the American forests and by the creation of dusty arid fields where once there was verdant prairie.

Another American bird that has benefited from the spread of farms and fields is the Cowbird. This bird belongs to the Icteridae, a family of mainly rather starling-like American birds, to which the American orioles, American blackbirds and the meadowlarks (none of which bears any close relation to their Old-World namesakes) also belong. The Cowbird looks rather like a smallish, stocky, thick-billed Starling with a black body and brown head; the female is a dull, dark grey. It is parasitic, like our Cuckoo, and lays its eggs in the nests of many species of birds, particularly those of many of the American warblers.

The Cowbird was originally a bird of the prairies where it accompanied grazing herds of Buffaloes (to give the American Bison their popular if zoologically incorrect name) and fed partly on insects disturbed by them. Like other birds which follow large grazing animals for this purpose, such as the Starling and Yellow Wagtail, it readily switched to domestic cattle when these replaced the wild herds. Man has cut down the forests of eastern North America in some places, and created fields and open spaces everywhere; the Cowbird has spread east and its range now extends to the eastern seaboard. Although it makes use of large grazing animals when available, it can manage without their help and I found it common in all the more open parts of the woodlands around New York in May 1962.

One drawback of the Cowbird's success in following in man's footsteps is that this has brought it into contact with species, such as the rare Kirtland's Warbler, which have previously been free of nest parasites and are not yet adapted to surviving with them. There is some evidence to suggest that the Cowbird may be having a more detrimental effect on some of these newly-parasitised eastern species than it did on those in its original home – or, one might better say on those which had managed to thrive in spite of its attentions there, for it is possible that, before man came on the scene, some species or other may have become extinct because it could not cope with the Cowbird's parasitism in addition to other hazards of existence.

The Lapwing is another bird whose range man has undoubtedly increased. We are inclined to think of man as an enemy to this most beautiful of all the world's plovers; until recent years it was widely killed for food in Britain and its eggs systematically collected for sale as a luxury. In some other countries the Lapwing is shot for food and in many of its breeding places agricultural work leads too often to the accidental destruction of numberless clutches of its eggs and broods of its chicks. However, but for man the Lapwing would not exist in many of these areas at all! It is a bird of the open wastes, fields and pastures. Most of these, at least in Britain and western Europe, were originally forest land where no Lapwings could have lived. The Lapwing was probably a bird of the less fertile parts of the grasslands of eastern Europe and Asia, and perhaps of fairly open marshes, large shingle bars in rivers and similar habitats elsewhere. It is still found abundantly in such places, where they exist, but is now primarily, at least with us, a bird of the farmlands.

In America the Lapwing's place is partly taken by a very different plover, the Killdeer. This is one of the 'ringed plover' group although not at all a typical member of it. It is rather like our Ringed Plover in colour but is a warmer, more buffy brown above and has two black bands around its white breast instead of one. It is also larger than the Ringed Plover although not quite so large as a Lapwing. It inhabits much the same sort of places in North America as the Lapwing does in Europe and Asia, and must likewise have been enabled to increase its range as man destroyed the forest and where his open fields replaced it.

The Rook is often thought of as one of the most characteristic birds of the British countryside. So it is, at least of the agricultural countryside; it is not usually found in extensive built-up areas nor in completely wild country as is its more versatile relative the Carrion Crow. It is, however, unlikely that there were any Rooks in Britain, or indeed in western Europe, before there were any farmers. The Rook must originally have been a bird of the grassy steppes of Europe and Asia where it foraged widely over the land in search of insects, worms and seeds, and made the most of the few available patches of woodland or scrub by nesting colonially.

When grain-growing man invaded its living space the Rook must soon have discovered that ploughing exposed large supplies of earthworms, grubs, insects and the occasional small mammal, and that the grain which he sowed was bigger and better than most of the wild grass seeds. As man spread into the western forests, felling them to make fields, the Rook followed him and became a familiar farm-land bird throughout much of Europe.

In England dislike of the Rook's pilfering of sown grain and (in pre-combine harvester days) its pulling cornstacks to bits in hard weather has never led to really concerted efforts to exterminate it. Since the means of extermination have been available in the form of guns and modern poisons, there have always been many people who liked the Rook and did not want to see it banished from our countryside. So the local and usually sporadic attacks on rookeries have had little or no permanent effect on its numbers. The situation has been very different in some countries where there was no popular sentiment in favour of the bird and where it was, as a result, wiped out as a breeding species from many areas.

Water in the desert

The recent exceptionally dry summer of 1976 notwithstanding, water in Britain is usually plentiful, much too plentiful we often think when it rains on a day we go bird-watching! Thus we do not usually consider how its presence or absence can affect the distribu-tion of birds other than aquatic or riparian species like reed warblers, ducks, grebes or kingfishers. The situation is very different in many arid countries. In these there are often plentiful, widespread supplies of food, at least for seed-eating birds, as seeds often lie in good condi-tion on or in the bare dusty ground for months or even years until rain comes and they germinate, if they have not been eaten in the meantime. Water is, however, often in short supply. Drinking places may be few and far between and in dry years most of them may dry up. Those birds that need to drink regularly can only live where they are within easy flying distance of surface water and are unable to inhabit vast areas that would supply them with food but no drink. Many arid-country birds are able to go without drinking for long periods and some do not drink even when water is available. Others, such as the parrots, pigeons, sandgrouse, weavers, estrildids or grass-finches, and the crows, must have water; although some of the sandgrouse and at least one species each of weavers and estrildids can live for a long time without it, as has, I regret to say, been discovered by cruel experiments.

Man must have water for himself and his livestock. This means that wherever man lives or travels in dry country he has dug wells or made other sources of water available. To what extent these can be used by birds depends much on circumstances, particularly on how tolerant the people are of the birds sharing their drinking supply. More often than not, however, such places provide water for birds as well as men. On the arid coastal plains of Eritrea and Somaliland, African Collared Doves, the ancestors of our domestic Barbary Dove, gather in hundreds around the native wells; Rock Pigeons in arid parts of India will sometimes fly down into wells and alight on the water for a moment to drink if there is no handy ledge from which they can reach the surface.

When, in 1965, I was in the arid interior of Australia, I was able to see how some of the birds there benefited from man's water supplies. Although much of the country, at least in dry seasons, does not look to English eyes as if it would support a camel, much less a cow, great numbers of cattle and horses are run on it – indeed horses have in many parts become feral and are looked on as vermin. Wherever the land is part of a 'cattle station' one finds windmills that pump up the underground water and keep an adjacent cattle trough filled. It will give an idea of how much artificial water supplies are used by birds if I describe the birds that came to one such trough. This was in the north-west of interior South Australia, quite close to the 'red centre' and much of the surrounding sandy soil was rich orange-red in colour. It was all dotted with acacia trees, Mulga scrub as it is called, with a few other shrubs and here and there, but not anywhere very near the trough, were dry creeks lined with great gum trees whose white trunks and pale grey-green leaves contrasted vividly with the blue sky.

The trough stood at the foot of the big round iron tank beside a creaking metal windmill in an enclosed stockade. This was used to trap feral horses. Normally all the gates were open, but in the hot summer they were closed and only a small, spiked entrance left in the stockade through which a thirst-crazed horse could push its way in but could not get out, on the familiar lobster pot principle.

Before daylight, indeed when only a grey hint of dawn was in the eastern sky, came the first birds, the lovely little Bourke's Parakeets. They arrived with a swift flickering rattle of wings and soft chirruping calls, like some of the calls of the familiar Budgerigar but softer, that seemed to sound suddenly from everywhere at once as the birds darted, waist-high, through the scrub. As it grew a little lighter one could make out their trim little forms, running about on the ground near the trough, flying up on to it, taking sip after sip and then speeding away. By the time it was light enough to see clearly all had usually gone but one day three came in late, almost half an hour after sunrise, and I was able to enjoy the full beauty of this most delicately-coloured parrot – the bright Cambridge-blue rumps and outer tail feathers, the deeper blue under their wings as they flitted nervously around before alighting on the stockade fence and then flying down to the trough, and the delicate shell pink of their bellies.

Shortly after sunrise a pair of Mulga Parrots – the 'Many-coloured Parakeet' of English aviculturists – alighted suddenly on the fence. The cock with his brilliant green plumage, marked with orange, yellow, red and blue, lives up to his English name. Seeing a skin in a museum or even a painting, one can have the impression that the bird is almost too gaudy. But alive, running along the fence top and then down on to the trough, he looked entirely beautiful, a vivid jewel in a rather drab setting, and his more quietly-clad mate in her mainly olive plumage made a perfect foil for his brilliance.

While the Mulga Parrots were drinking a little party of Crested Pigeons had arrived and perched on a dead, hawthorn-like looking tree about fifty metres away. Judging from the behaviour of other Crested Pigeons that I watched coming to drink elsewhere, these would have perched much nearer to the water but for the fact that there was no suitable tree close to the trough. Here they waited uttering their distress call – a soft musical 'oo' – an expression of their inner conflict between desire to drink and fear of going down to the water. This is always a dangerous thing to do as the local birds of prey are apt to hang around water points to try to catch drinking birds. Indeed, natural sources of water themselves may harbour snapping turtles or crocodiles liable to seize an unwary bird.

In pairs and little parties more Crested Pigeons arrived until there were about forty on the tree top. One took wing and with a long glide, interspersed with a quick whistling rattle of its wings, flew to the trough and perched on the fence above; others streamed after it and one after another they flew down and drank deeply, each as it finished drinking flying away in the direction from which it had come.

From time to time during the day a slim, grey-green Singing Honeyeater suddenly flew out of the tangle of bushes just behind the tank and sipped quickly before flying back into cover. The dainty little Diamond Dove was another bird that came in the heat of the day, unlike the other pigeons. I never saw crows come to this trough, perhaps because we were camping near it and they were not numerous in the district, but at other water I saw them come at different times of day although in each case the crows saw me before reaching the water, became suspicious when they saw my eyes focus on them and flew off at once without drinking, leaving me feeling rather guilty at having scared them away.

In the evening came a few Crested Pigeons, whether some of the same individuals who had drunk that morning I don't know. Then, heralding their appearance with shrill cries, a great flock of some hundreds of Roseate Cockatoos, Galahs to the Australian, that lined up on the stockade like rows of moving silver-grey and rose-pink blossoms on the dead wood. While they were still drinking came the wailing cries of a pair of the larger and even more beautiful Pink Cockatoos, snow-white with delicate pink underparts and a rich deeper pink flush under their wings. When they settled they raised their brilliant red and yellow banded crests in momentary alarm before flying down to the trough.

Before the cockatoos arrived a soft but penetrating 'oom, oom', like the lowing of some distant but deep-voiced cow, sounding intermittently from some thickish scrub about two hundred metres away, indicated that the birds that would be last to drink, the

Bronzewing Pigeons, had begun to gather. I had heard and seen none in flight so possibly these were local birds that had spent the day quite near. The sun slid lower, slipped below the horizon, the gloom gathered and suddenly the air was filled with the beat of pigeons' wings as the big, heavy birds came flying low and fast through the Mulga scrub. Occasionally in the dying light one settled at once near to the trough but most alighted in cover a hundred metres or more away. Besides the rush and flap of Bronzewings there were also here and there the rattling wings and soft chirruping of Bourke's Parakeets, but these were not in such numbers as in the morning. It was

Roseate Cockatoos or Galahs at a cattle trough. In some arid areas this beautiful and abundant cockatoo relies largely on water provided by man for his domestic animals.

nearly dark and, straining my eyes, I could suddenly see a phalanx of pigeons, dozens upon dozens of them, not line abreast but in little hesitant groups, walking over the open ground and converging towards the trough. I think that they did not see well in the very dim light, for they walked with their heads not nodding to and fro but held straight forward, as a Domestic Pigeon does when it is forced to walk in darkness. They were nervous and alert; each bird would take a dozen or so paces then stop. Each time one stopped its nervousness affected others, which stopped also, each time one moved forwards others were encouraged to follow. The trough was now in deep shadow and I could only hear, not see what happened there, but I know my ears interpreted rightly from having watched Bronzewings at a natural water hole on a small hill top where, silhouetted against the skyline, they could be seen, to some extent, as well as heard. As each bird flew up to the trough it drank deeply. The moment its thirst was quenched it flew swiftly and noisily away.

Few things in bird life have more impressed me than the contrast between the Bronzewing Pigeon's slow, cautious, hesitating walk the last few hundred metres to water and its impetuous flight away from the drinking place the moment it has assuaged its thirst. I do not think it is being anthropomorphic to believe that a Bronzewing Pigeon coming to drink *is* as apprehensive as it appears to be and that it must experience great relief as it flies back to the relative safety of its distant home in the scrub. Drinking before dawn or after sunset, as Bourke's Parakeet and the Bronzewing Pigeon do, probably serves to lessen the chances of being caught by hawks or falcons which, in dry countries, hunt by day around water supplies. It also enables them to avoid flying to and from water during the intense heat of the day.

This particular trough was not patronised by Zebra Finches as there were none in its neighbourhood, but at most other water points that I saw in inland Australia this species was the most abundant visitor. I vividly remember one such place in the interior of Western Australia not far from Warburton. Here the Zebra Finches drank from and bathed in a shallow muddy puddle of water that spread around the base of the leaky storage tank below the windmill. Throughout the day there was a constant coming and going of flock after flock of the bright, noisy little estrildids. Around the tank each of the few scrubby bushes and scraggy Mulga trees was literally alive with hundreds of Zebra Finches, the ground beneath white with their droppings.

The smell and the noise of the calling of possibly thousands, of the nasal-sounding, 'tin-trumpet' voiced birds put me in mind of some overcrowded bird dealer's – only more so, much more so! I had the impression that each Zebra Finch drank more than once at each visit and spent some time bathing, preening and resting before flying home. This bird, like the pigeons and parrots, is one of the species that will indicate the whereabouts of water to the traveller, and as it visits its drinking places at all hours, he will not have to wait till evening as he may with other species.

In other arid countries similar use is made by birds of man's water supplies. Over large areas of South West Africa, for example, sand-grouse, doves and lovebirds are now more widespread and abundant than they were before the white man settled the land and installed wells, pumps and water-pipes. A local bird-watcher observed that in many of the drier parts of South West Africa not only every open well and trough but even every leaking outside water tap was visited by scores, and in some cases by hundreds of birds daily.

There can, of course, be dangers in sharing man's water supply. Sportsmen lurk around both artificial and natural drinking places to shoot pigeons and sandgrouse coming to drink. Primitive peoples often, with more justification, snare and trap birds under such conditions. A less obvious danger from man's water supplies, but one likely to be very detrimental in the long run, is that man's domestic animals, especially goats and sheep, may prevent the regeneration of trees and shrubs on which the birds rely for food. This seems to be happening in parts of Australia where, as has long been the case over much of the Scottish highlands, sheep eat all the young trees as soon as they appear.

Highways and byeways

Most mammals, from the herds of bison that formerly migrated across the North American prairies to the grey squirrel running and leaping along its accustomed way through the trees to our bird-table, go about their affairs by precise and largely unvarying routes. Usually such routes are soon so modified by the passage of their feet and bodies, sometimes also by more deliberate actions, that even we humans who seldom notice the scent signs that usually also mark them, can recognise the 'run' of the creature concerned. We ourselves, in our usual way, surpass most other mammals in our passion for making paths and roadways and all of them in our ability to do so.

In so far as they destroy part of the former habitat, paths and roads, like all other human artefacts, must of necessity do harm to the interests of some wild creatures. The invention of the internal combustion engine brought an altogether new era for most of the species who use (man-made) roads and yearly claims its holocaust of victims, human and otherwise. Also, as they bring man and his works into areas previously free or relatively free from them, roads are therefore ultimately harmful to birds that cannot thrive alongside man. Here, however, I shall discuss primarily ways in which some birds exploit and benefit from the presence of paths, tracks and roads. First considering mainly the types of paths, tracks and 'old-fashioned' roads with which those of us no longer young have been familiar from early childhood and then the modern motorways.

From a bird's-eye view the most important common feature of almost all paths, tracks or roads is that they provide an area of bare or nearly bare ground, sometimes less than a metre across, sometimes quite wide, and always of considerable linear extent. I am naturally including macadamised, paved or concreted areas as 'bare ground' just as the birds do. These bare areas are often far from unproductive for the birds. Insects and other small creatures attempt to cross them, other insects and seeds are blown on to or fall upon them. On the bare surface both seeds and insects can be more easily spotted by the birds than they usually can be among the surrounding herbage or

leaf litter. So that although there may be actually fewer seeds or insects on the path or road than on a comparable area of the neighbour-
ing field, woodland floor or whatever, they will often be much more
readily available. Hence many individuals of many bird species habitually feed in such places. In Britain Chaffinches, Song Thrushes,
Blackbirds, Robins, Dunnocks and even Pied Wagtails often prefer
to gather up fallen caterpillars on the road beneath the trees than
to search for them among the leaves. Yellow Buntings and Reed
Buntings habitually feed on paths and tracks that bisect their habitats,
gleaning mostly fallen seeds of grasses but also taking insects in spring
and summer. Nor is it, incidentally, only the familiar birds that have
otherwise adapted to our man-altered surroundings that do this.
Where man-made paths or tracks run through really wild country
many of the ground-feeding birds take advantage of them. When
I was in wild hill forest in eastern Brazil, I regularly heard the
hauntingly sad-sounding cooing of the Grey-fronted Dove from un-
seen birds among the undergrowth but the only place I saw them,
and that regularly, was seeking food on tracks through the forest.

Roads or broad tracks running through woodland also create artificial glades and openings, narrow, but extensive in length. This
enables species that normally inhabit openings within, or the edge of
forest, to increase their range. In Britain the Spotted Flycatcher often
hunts insects in, or rather above roads running through woods, just
as it does in the glades and openings that are its natural summer habitat, and in the tree-screened gardens that it has secondarily colonised.
Anyone who walks much in wooded country will know that visually
and otherwise, but especially visually, a man-made track or road running through woodland has much in common with a stream flowing
through it, except, of course, that water, apart from occasional
puddles perhaps, is not usually present. Species that often or habitually forage along the sides of such streams are sometimes attracted,
presumably because of the similarity in general aspects, to roads
through woods or forests. In Britain both Pied and Grey Wagtails
are sometimes seen running about catching insects on a woodland
road or path (and, as has been said, the former species regularly feeds
on tree-shaded roads within its usual haunts). When in Brazil in the

autumn of 1972 I was surprised one morning to come upon a Spotted Sandpiper, a species very similar in appearance and habits to the old world Common Sandpiper, on a road through the forest. When I got too near for its liking it took wing, flying ahead of me on decurved wings low over the road just as it and the Common Sandpiper do over the surface of a stream or river.

For ground-feeding birds, especially those that run or walk, the surfaces of roads and paths are often much 'easier going' than those of the surrounding areas. This is especially but not only so when these are densely-planted crops, such as wheat or maize at an advanced stage. Game-birds such as grouse, partridges and pheasants and waders, such as some plovers and coursers, are very fond of bringing their young chicks on to paths and tracks where both adults and young can move easily and keep each other readily in view.

Foods that get on to roads in the natural way of things may be unintentionally 'processed' by man into suitable form for some birds. Chaffinches, for example, are fond of beechmast but seem usually to have difficulty in coping with the tough-shelled triangular nuts unless their husks have been broken or softened. Where beech trees overhang a road the problem is solved for them by the traffic. When the trees have borne a good crop, Chaffinches, tits (which can and do hack the nuts open but often prefer to have the job done for them), and sometimes also Dunnocks and Collared Doves, visit the road beneath them to feed on the crushed and broken kernels. Sweet chestnuts, which are of no use to small or weak-billed birds in their natural freshly-ripened state are also readily eaten when crushed on the roadway. It is now usually car and lorry wheels that provide this service but in former days cartwheels doubtless served as well.

Grain that has been accidentally spilled during transit is another source of food for some birds, from Eastern Rock Pigeons and Snow Pigeons gleaning on tracks high in the Himalayas to House Sparrows feasting 'between cars' on grain spilled on some country road in England. In general such spillage tends to be more regular and predictable in those countries where beasts of burden or human carriers are still in use than in those where motor vehicles are used. Use of the latter does, indeed, result in a surprisingly large amount of grain being spilled but often rather unpredictably so that, although it may provide a windfall for such local birds as discover it, it is not even a seasonably reliable food source.

The dung of horses and other beasts of burden often contains some undigested grain which thus becomes available for birds. In the 1930s, when there were still large numbers of horse-drawn vehicles in London and its suburbs, I often saw House Sparrows and Feral Pigeons picking grains from horse droppings. That most deservedly popular of natural history writers, Gilbert White, was, I believe, the first bird-watcher to see and record Carrion Crows actually eating horse dung itself, when pressed for food in hard weather. A prettier and less well-known member of the Crow family – Biddulph's Ground Jay of Central Asia – also eats horse dung, although it appears not to be known whether or not it does so only in times of shortage of other foods.

Where cars and lorries have replaced beasts of burden this source of food is no longer available but a different and to many of us far less pleasing one is supplied by the corpses of mammals and birds killed by the traffic. Birds of prey, especially the scavenging Black Kite, some gulls and crows often feed on such casualties, sometimes at great risk to themselves. During the hard winter of 1962/3, it was reported that a hare was run over on a motorway in central Europe. In the course of the next week or two several Kites and a larger number of Buzzards suffered the same fate as they fed on its remains, or attempted to do so. It is not only species that normally feed partly or wholly on vertebrate animals that exploit this rich if risky source of protein food. In Australia the introduced Spicebird, a seed-eating estrildid 'finch', regularly eats the crushed and more or less dehydrated remains of small mammals and birds killed on the roads. An Australian ornithologist and writer, who investigated the matter, published his findings in the *Victorian Naturalist*, June 1962. It is extremely likely that many other small birds take this new source of food even though they do not seem to have been recorded doing so, perhaps because we tend to assume a small bird seen feeding on the road must be taking only seeds or insects.

Paths, tracks and roads are, of course, all sources of grit for some birds, especially if we include as grit not only the small stones that many seed-eating birds swallow and which appear to aid the grinding of their food in their gizzards but also the bits of limestone, snail shell and other mineral matter which they also take to obtain calcium and possibly other minerals. Earth that contains various salts, and salt itself, at any rate when more or less diluted and mixed with earth or sand, is eaten by some species of doves and finches. In many towns and suburbs in England, the local authorities have placed bunkers of salt for use on the road in case of sudden freezing spells. Sooner or later, a strong solution of salt seeps out of such containers and spreads around their base, more or less crystallising in dry weather and remaining or becoming wet when it is damp. I have often seen Feral Pigeons eating this diluted salt. They seem to do so most often just after dawn and before they have fed, apparently taking the salt on an empty stomach, just as at Weymouth (and doubtless other seaside towns) some of them fly down to the tide's edge and eat the wet sand *before* going to look for their breakfast.

The puddles formed on modern roads are usually ephemeral and much polluted but on or beside more 'primitive' roads, tracks and bridle-paths puddles or small pools may last for several weeks even in dry weather. I know of one bridle-path on the North Downs near Guildford, England, that runs through woodland and scrub where there are no streams, ponds or other surface water. At one point where it is well shaded its puddles often hold water even in late spring and summer and, if one sits quietly at a little distance and watches through binoculars, one sees a surprising variety of woodland birds come to drink and bathe. Trackside and roadside puddles are also often used by species that need mud for their nests, in Britain by the House Martin and Swallow in open areas and by Song Thrush and Blackbird in woodland. Paths, tracks and earth roads often provide the sort of finely-powdered dusty earth that may not be available in the fields, woods or gardens on either side. Hence many birds that dustbathe habitually visit such tracks or paths to do so. Skylarks in Britain and Hoopoes in Egypt are the species that I recall most often seeing dusting themselves in such situations. With the shyer (because more persecuted) gamebirds one is more likely to find only the unmistakable signs of the recent dust bath, often with one or two body feathers to indicate for certain which species was involved. On the only occasion in my life when I have had a really clear view of a Wren dustbathing, it was doing so in the middle of a woodland path.

Modern motorways are a far cry from woodland paths or even from the meandering and still extant country roads of yesteryear. They offer fewer and more dangerous opportunities for birds to feed on the road itself but they offer some advantages of their own. These are their wide grass verges and embankments on which most of the grass or other herbage is kept fairly short, and areas of grass, shrubs or trees surrounded by or adjacent to the highway, and comparative freedom from humans or dogs on foot. In England Rooks, Jackdaws, Carrion Crows and many smaller species habitually feed on motorway verges, unperturbed by the traffic passing close to them. The Kestrel is one of the most characteristic 'motorway birds', as the extensive sloping embankments and grassy verges provide not only good numbers of insects and small mammals but good opportunities for seeing and catching them. Hence hovering Kestrels are a common sight along many motorways, catching the eye of all motorists who take even a casual interest in the wildlife around them.

Even for those birds which most use the amenities they offer, paths and roads may have some disadvantages. So far as natural, or perhaps one had better say 'non-human' dangers are concerned most man-made roads or paths present no greater hazards than do alternative feeding or drinking places, where the unwary, weak or inexperienced bird is just as likely to be ambushed by a hawk, cat or other lurking predator. A possible exception may be sunken lanes in wooded or partly-wooded country which seem to offer exceptionally favourable hunting opportunities for such hawks as the Sparrowhawk. The case is otherwise, however, with human predation. Paths, tracks and minor roads usually contribute much to the success of the human predator, whether he is a native child setting a snare for a dove he has seen feeding on the forest path or a sportsman, gun in hand, in pursuit of 'feathered vermin'.

On modern roads traffic constitutes a more or less constant threat of death, although birds probably suffer less than many other forms of wildlife. In Britain I think the Hedgehog and the Common Toad must have proportionately heavier casualties than any other vertebrates. Birds do, however, suffer many casualties, especially the inexperienced juveniles. It is probably at least as much a matter of the killing off of most of those young birds whose initial responses to traffic are 'wrong' than of the birds learning as they get older. Although birds normally avoid any large object that comes directly at them, moving vehicles supply few factors in common with natural predators and, since birds are usually killed by them or escape unscathed, they are not likely to *learn* any great fear of them. Adult birds that have lived a year or more near busy roads all too often literally fly into danger from traffic unheeding it, when they are being chased in a territorial or sexual pursuit or are suddenly startled. When birds not much used to traffic (and therefore that have not undergone any 'weeding out' in youth) and/or which are weak from hunger come to close quarters with it, their casualties are often high.

In winter in England, during periods of snow, many Redwings and other thrushes are attracted to roads by the sight of a snow-free substrate. Where there is a grass verge they then often find that, immediately adjacent to the road, the ground at the edge of the verge is snow-free, so they spend much time there searching for food. Should a footpath run along a metre or so from the road's edge, people using the path usually do not see, and are not themselves seen by the foraging bird until they are nearly upon it. The bird, suddenly startled, flies away across the road and too often is hit by a car as it does so. During a short cold spell at Tring in Hertfordshire, England, in the winter of 1975, I myself accidentally caused a Redwing's death like this. In the few days that this hard spell lasted from four to six Redwings and one or two Song Thrushes and Blackbirds were killed each day on this half-kilometre stretch of road, probably in the same manner.

Motor vehicles have been particularly damaging to birds, and I should guess in all probability to humans as well, when they have become abundant during a very short period of time in places where they were previously absent or rare and where birds had been accustomed to no such hazards when feeding on the roads. In some towns in south-east Asia the Spotted Dove has, it is said, been reduced to a fraction of its former numbers from this cause.

A place to nest

'Thou Dove who art in the cleft of the Rock and in the secret places under the Stairs!' Those who read the Bible as well as bird books will know this line from the Song of Solomon. Its composer was evidently sufficiently appreciative of the beauty of the Rock Pigeon (or Rock Dove) to deem it a fit comparison for his beloved. Also, and of more interest to us at present, it shows that then, as now, Rock Pigeons in the Middle East were making use of both natural and man-made nest sites. Many kinds of birds nest in caves, on sheltered rock ledges, on overhung rock faces and similar places. Since earliest times, or at least the earliest times for which we have written records, man has supplied some of these species with alternative and additional nest sites and by so doing has often greatly affected their distribution and increased their numbers.

The swallows, or some of them, are always associated in our minds with human dwellings. Not only do they breed about farms and villages in most temperate and tropical parts of the world but they are almost everywhere looked upon with favour by the human inhabitants. Often this may now be due to superstitious or religious feeling, swallows being reckoned lucky birds to have about the place or to be special favourites of gods or saints so that it is unlucky to kill them. It is, however, likely that such superstitions, and the many favourable legends in which swallows figure, grew up *after* the birds had become favourites, not before. Incidentally, although some swallows are called martins, the species so-called are not all particularly closely related to each other. The British Swallow is, for example, much more closely related to the Crag Martin than the House Martin is to the Sand Martin.

The Swallow of Britain was originally a bird that nested in caves and under rock overhangs. It built its open-topped half- or part-bowl-shaped nest, or at least started to build it, on some ledge or projection that would give a little support, although if it found an otherwise suitable site without any little ledge, outcrop or projecting root to start from it would sometimes build straight out from the vertical rock face. In Europe and Asia there are relatively few places where the Swallow can find suitable natural nesting sites. Far more often it now nests, and for long has nested, inside barns, cowsheds, out-houses and other buildings that serve as 'artificial caves'. In former days in Britain and elsewhere it often nested inside the big, old-fashioned chimneys, hence its former name of 'Chimney Swallow' and its still current German name 'Rauchschwalbe' (Smoke Swallow). Gilbert White, in his evergreen masterpiece *The Natural History of Selborne*, gives a vivid description of its methods of entering and leaving the chimney. Where people do not object, the Swallow will nest freely inside human dwellings. When I was in Cairo I saw breeding Swallows, there of the dark, chestnut-bellied Egyptian race of the species, darting in and out of doorways in the poorer parts of the town. One could often see people sitting at the tables outside some eating place, sipping their coffee while Swallows flew in and out fearlessly over their heads.

In North America, the same species, there called the Barn Swal-low, has also taken to nesting in buildings. Indeed the only place where I have ever seen the Swallow nesting in a natural site was Aus-tralia. There, on the Nullarbor plain, I found Swallows nesting on sheltered projections and ledges in small potholes in open country. I may say that there is some disagreement as to whether the Austra-lian Welcome Swallow should be considered as a race of the Swallow (which it certainly appeared to me to be) or as a good species. Its habits so far as nesting is concerned are identical and it has also taken widely to nesting inside buildings.

Another swallow that nests on buildings is the House Martin, Shakespeare's 'temple-haunting martlet' familiar to Macbeth-addicts. This species usually builds on an outside wall, making a half- or part-cup of mud built up to the overhanging eaves, leaving a shallow hole for entrance. Although it usually builds from a vertical wall to an overhang, it particularly likes a situation where some support is given at the side as well, doubtless because the nest is both easier to build and takes less time to finish in such a situation.

A House Martin building. This familiar British bird is one of several species of swallows which have increased in numbers along with man through using his buildings as nest sites and thus no longer being dependent on the presence of suitable overhung cliffs. (*John Heywood*)

Although the House Martin now nests mostly on buildings, it seems more often to use natural sites than the Swallow does. Probably this is because cliffs with suitable niches and overhangs are more common than caves, at least in Britain and western Europe. Indeed in one respect at least the natural site has the advantage. When it is nesting on a cliff the House Martin nearly always seeks the mud for its nest above the cliff top, on the higher ground. So when it is carrying the great blob of mud back to the nest it only has to fly, or rather for the most part glide, downwards, whereas when nesting under the eaves it has to make an upward flight with each load.

Many other species of swallows, in different parts of the world, that naturally build mud nests attached to cliffs or caves have taken extensively to building on or in human dwellings. There are, however, some swallows, like our Sand Martin (called Bank Swallow in North America), which dig tunnels in a vertical or nearly vertical bank to nest in and others which just nest in any suitable hole or niche in a tree, bank or cliff. Both these groups have also profited through man. All of the Sand Martin colonies that I have seen in England and America, for example, have been in the sides of sandpits excavated by man, often far from any natural bank where the birds could have nested. The Sand Martin breeds widely in Asia, Africa and North America as well as in Europe; like the Swallow, it was a widespread and successful species before man came on the scene but there can be little doubt that he has been instrumental in further increasing its numbers and range.

Of the swallows that normally nest in natural holes in trees, cliffs or banks the one that has probably benefited most from man is the Purple Martin. This is a large North American swallow about the size of an English Swift. The male is a glossy bluish-purplish-black and the female mainly dark grey. It has long been the custom to put out nest boxes or hollow gourds on posts for it to nest in. This seems at one time to have been done largely for utilitarian purposes; the martins by persistently mobbing any hawk or crow that came near their nests helped to protect their benefactor's chickens. Most of the multiple-compartment 'martin houses', in which the majority of these birds probably now nest, are erected because of affection or aesthetic appreciation; although, handsome as the Purple Martin is, I can assure my English readers that the British House Martin is, at least to my way of thinking, a prettier and more delightful creature! Incidentally, an American species that looks rather like it, the Tree Swallow, now often breeds in nest boxes and in 'martin houses' that have failed to attract Purple Martins.

The swifts are not related to swallows, and only tend to look like them because they also are adapted to spending a lot of time flying about without alighting and to catching insects on the wing. Swifts nest in various places, most typically either in holes of some sort or in caves. Their nests are usually rather scanty affairs, built of such materials as they can find floating about in the air, which they gum together with a sticky secretion produced from their mouths. In the Edible Nest Swift the translucent whitish nest stuck on the side of a cave is made entirely from this saliva. It is a luxury food of the Chinese, who have superstitious and almost certainly untrue beliefs about its supposed near-magical properties. As a result the collecting of its nests from the caves in south-east Asia, where it breeds, has long been big business.

Many swifts in different parts of the world have taken to nesting in or on buildings, either directly or by dispossessing swallows of the mud nests they have already built. I will here mention two species of swift which have benefited greatly from mankind, one or other of which will be familiar to a majority of readers of this book.

The British Swift is widespread as a breeding bird throughout most of Europe. Originally a nester in holes in cliffs and trees, the Swift has, over most of its range, taken to nesting in holes and crevices in buildings. It tends to feed higher in the air than the swallows usually do and it will travel further from its nest site to collect food. Hence the Swift is less affected by the various factors that tend to make many insects scarce in and around towns, for the high-flying or rather high-drifting insects on which it largely feeds are often wind-borne from some way off and, when there are few insects above the town, the Swifts will fly to a distance to hunt. They are, therefore, usually much more abundant in and above towns than swallows.

It is interesting to watch Swifts looking for nest sites. It seems amazing that they can discover the various small holes and narrow crevices they nest in when flying past the building at speed, even though they fly up to the entrance and away again many times before they first enter. As with other hole nesting species, such as the Feral Pigeon and Stock Dove, they are often initially attracted by a dark patch or shadow on the building that only *appears*, from a little distance, to be a hole or crevice. It is interesting that both avian and human eyes can be similarly deceived in this way. The Swift makes its nest of bits of straw, feathers, the 'winged' seeds of elm and other trees

A Swift bringing food, carried in its throat, to its young in a derelict barn. In Britain and most of Europe many more Swifts nest in buildings than in natural sites in rock crevices or tree holes. (*C. C. Doncaster*)

and anything of that sort that it finds floating about in the air. These it cements together with saliva into a rather poor-looking, roughly saucer-shaped nest.

When English chimneys were commonly wider, Swallows used, as has been said, to nest regularly in them, but they seldom do so today. Chimneys are, however, now the usual nesting place for a common swift in North America – the Chimney Swift. This is a dull little blackish-grey swift about the size of a Sand Martin; in the air it looks rather like a fat little cigar with wings on. Originally it nested in hollow trees, especially large dead trunks open at the top, but nowadays it nests most commonly in chimneys although also in barns and other buildings. The nest consists of a frail-looking shallow half-saucer, or perhaps better half-basket, of small dead twigs stuck together and to the side of the chimney or tree hollow with saliva. The young leave the nest before they can fly and then spend their time clinging to the wall.

Besides nesting in chimneys the Chimney Swift also roosts in them. On migration great flocks often roost in large, tall chimneys which they circle above and finally enter in a huge funnel formation at dusk. It is probable that for this species large tall chimneys, open only at the top, supply a 'supra-normal stimulus' to the Chimney Swift's instinctive 'judgment', which of course evolved in relation to natural sites. No doubt the dead tree that came nearest to a factory chimney – as tall as possible, open only at the top – was the safest sort of tree in which to nest and roost . Chimneys are by no means always safe but on the whole the Chimney Swift must have benefited by using them and probably now exists in far greater numbers than it did before modern civilisation came to eastern North America.

At the beginning of this section the Rock Pigeon was mentioned as a species that early took to nesting in buildings. It is, I think, probable that the first step in the domestication of this pigeon was taken by the bird itself when it began to nest in houses as well as in caves. It is of interest that of the four related species of pigeons with similar nesting habits, three have also taken to nesting in buildings on quite a large scale. Over much of central and eastern Asia the Eastern Rock Pigeon replaces the Rock Pigeon. Where not persecuted – this is happily the case throughout much of its range – it often nests in buildings. It is very similar to the Rock Pigeon, from which it chiefly differs in appearance by having a white band across its tail.

The Speckled Pigeon is found over much of tropical and southern Africa. In a natural state it nests in hollows in trees or cliffs. In many places it has now taken to nesting in or on buildings. It is a handsome bird with purplish-chestnut, white-spotted wings, shining pinkish-bronze or pinkish-silver bifurcated neck feathers that it erects in a frieze round its head when giving its bowing display, and bare red skin around its eyes. It is very hardy and breeds freely in captivity, so it is often to be seen in zoos and private aviaries in Europe and America.

The White-collared Pigeon is dark grey with some black marks on its wing coverts, a white ring round the back of its neck and white patches on its wing that show only in flight or when the wings are opened. It is found only on the high plateaux and mountains of Ethiopia and Eritrea, where it nests in caves and recesses in cliffs. In

White-collared Pigeon on a stable roof in Addis Ababa. Like some other cave- and cliff-dwelling pigeons, this species has taken to nesting in buildings. It is a common and characteristic bird of the Ethiopian capital. (*Timothy Wylam*)

Addis Ababa it has not only taken to nesting in and on buildings but also to feeding in the streets and open spaces; indeed it behaves there much like Feral Pigeons do in London or New York.

The only one of these other four rock-nesting pigeons that does not nest in buildings is the Snow Pigeon. This is a bird of high altitudes in the Himalayas and although it feeds, at any rate in winter, largely in the cultivated valleys, it breeds and roosts high up, near or above the snow line.

Many of the birds that habitually nest in holes in buildings are species which under natural conditions will nest in any hole, whether in a tree or a cliff, provided it is of suitable size and seems reasonably safe – that is to say, provided they are not afraid of its immediate surroundings. Among British birds the Jackdaw and Starling come into this category. So, to a lesser extent, do the Tree Sparrow and the Stock Dove. The Tree Sparrow nests extensively in buildings throughout the eastern part of its world range although in England, and to a lesser extent elsewhere in Europe, it is a bird of the cultivated fields and waste land where it breeds in holes and crevices in the trees in nearby woods or groves. It is replaced in built-up areas and in farmyards and farm buildings by the House Sparrow.

Several related species of sparrows have taken to the House Sparrow's typical way of life but none of them seems able to compete with the House Sparrow in that sphere. It is usually only where the House Sparrow is absent that the Tree Sparrow, the Spanish Sparrow and the Desert Sparrow are able to live as 'house sparrows' in and around man's dwellings. Similarly, the Tree Sparrow would seem to be more successful in this niche than some of its relatives, although it cannot compete with the House Sparrow.

The Black Redstart was originally a bird that nested in holes and crevices in rocky banks or in inland or coastal cliffs, and similar places – unlike its more beautiful relative the Common Redstart which is a woodland bird and usually nests in holes in trees. Where they are nesting in natural sites the two species seldom occur together. Throughout most of central Europe, however, the Black Redstart now habitually nests in buildings, not only in such cliff-like structures as old ruins and castles but also in lowly cow-byres, barns and other outbuildings.

This has enabled the Black Redstart to become an abundant breeding species over large areas that would otherwise be unsuitable for it. Also as man has, in many places, cut openings in the woods, interspersed them with fields or grazing grounds, and scattered buildings here and there, so the Black Redstart has followed him, with the result that both these species of redstart can now be found commonly in the same environment. I found them both plentiful, but the Black Redstart much the more abundant, around the beautiful village of Seefeld in the Austrian Tyrol. It would be interesting to know whether the two compete at all for food. Probably there are enough insects for both in the breeding season, and in the winter they are not together because the Common Redstart migrates to tropical

Cock Black Redstart bringing food to nest. This originally rock-dwelling species now breeds largely in buildings. (*RSPB, Eric Hosking*)

Africa while the Black Redstart goes no further than the Mediterranean region and north Africa.

The Jackdaw, a bird that most British readers will be familiar with, is a neat little crow with a rather short bill, cheerful-sounding voice, silvery, silky nape and neck feathers and a striking whitish eye. Unlike most crows the Jackdaw nests in holes and sheltered nooks of all kinds, and readily nests in buildings when permitted to do so. In those parts of Britain and Europe where human tolerance of it is far from complete, the bird must, and does, regard man as a potential enemy. In such places Jackdaws usually nest only on high buildings such as churches. Where, however, they are not much interfered with they will nest in any sort of house, and indeed make themselves a nuisance by trying to nest inside chimneys, often coming to grief in the process.

The Jackdaw was probably originally a bird of fairly open country with either trees or cliffs (or both) where it could find holes large

Jackdaw with nesting material. Jackdaws often attempt to nest in the chimneys of occupied houses, usually without success. (*J. B. & S. Bottomley*)

enough in which to nest. It now lives mostly in cultivated regions where it often feeds largely on grain as well as on its natural foods of wild seeds and insects. It readily takes artificial food and in many places is a regular scavenger at rubbish tips. Where not molested it soon becomes bold enough to take food from lawns and bird-tables and in many places, for example parts of the south coast of Britain, it moves in as soon as a picnic party moves out and searches for edible scraps among the remaining litter.

In the far east the common Jackdaw is replaced by the closely-related Daurian Jackdaw, which differs in appearance by having the underparts and hind neck creamy white.

The Daurian Jackdaw behaves very like the Jackdaw and in some parts of its range nests in holes and crannies in buildings although in others, as in parts of eastern Tibet, it was said always to nest in holes in trees. This is not because of human persecution as in the same areas Choughs and Eastern Rock Pigeons nested freely in and about houses.

In some parts of its far-eastern range the Chough nests in buildings if allowed to do so. It has done the same on occasions in the Alps and the British Isles although it has in recent years declined in most western parts of its range and there seems, unfortunately, to be little hope that it will ever become a familiar bird of our towns.

Storks originally built their nests on trees, usually on fairly large and substantial ones, although also at times on large ledges of inland cliffs or the tops of large isolated rocks. However, over much of its range, especially in Europe and north-western Africa, the White Stork has for long nested chiefly on buildings. This striking white and black bird with its long red legs and bill has been a conspicuous figure in European folklore and loved and respected as an emblem of fertility, bringer of good luck, and symbol of filial piety. Legend tells how the Stork, hearing of Christ's birth, flew to Bethlehem and, finding him rather cold in the manger, plucked her own feathers to bed him more warmly. As a result she was the first to be blessed by the infant Jesus:

'Now blessèd be the gentle Stork
For ever more,' quoth he
'For that she saw my sad estate
And showèd such pity.
Full welcome shall she ever be
In Hamlet and in Hall
And ever called the blessèd Bird
And friend of Babies all.'

It is highly likely that by cutting down the forests and creating open spaces and at the same time supplying nesting sites (house tops) less liable to predation than sites in trees, man early made things easier in Europe for the White Stork which feeds in open marshes and grass-lands and, unlike its black relative, avoids woodlands. Furthermore, instead of being persecuted by man like most other large birds, the Stork was more usually loved and protected. It has long been the

custom, in some countries, to fix suitable nest sites – cartwheels, artificial nests, etc. – on or near roofs for Storks to nest on.

In recent years, however, things have taken a turn for the worse
for the Stork in Europe. In his latter-day 'progress' man has drained
much of the swampy land on which the Stork once found its food.
In Africa, where the bird winters, he has poisoned locusts by the mil-
lion and there is some reason to suppose that many Storks and other
birds have been thus indirectly poisoned, the White Stork being one
of the main bird predators on locust swarms in Africa. Perhaps most
important of all man has filled the European sky with wires, pylons
and other hazards which take a very large toll of Storks, particularly
of the inexperienced young when first on the wing. Finally, in some
of the Mediterranean countries where the Stork legend is less alive
White Storks are often shot on migration.

Thus although the White Stork, on its past history, perhaps merits
inclusion in this book as a bird of man's world it is no longer a
thriving one.

Under natural conditions the Kestrel nests – or at least lays its eggs,
for like other falcons it makes no more than a shallow scrape – in
cavities or on sheltered ledges of coastal or inland cliffs, hollows in
trees, or in the old nests of crows or other large birds. Where not
persecuted, it will readily nest in equivalent situations in buildings,
as it does regularly in both London and Cairo.

A closely-related species, the slightly smaller and rather more
brightly coloured Lesser Kestrel, commonly nests in buildings
throughout much of its range. This species is only a rare vagrant
to Britain but is an abundant summer resident in parts of southern
Europe and north-western Africa. There it regularly nests in holes
and crevices of buildings, often in colonies of several or even several
dozen pairs breeding close to one another and foraging in loose
flocks, for it is more sociable than its larger relative. Unlike the
Kestrel, which freely takes small birds, insects, lizards and other prey
but tends to concentrate on voles and mice where possible, the Lesser

Young White Storks on a nest built on a cartwheel, fixed for the purpose, on
a building in Jutland. (*C. C. Doncaster*)

A Kestrel at its nest site on the British Museum (Natural History), London. Note the eye and part of the head of one of the fledglings in the recess. (*Geoff Kinns*)

Kestrel is primarily an insect eater. This fact has enabled it to benefit further by its association with man. In many towns Lesser Kestrels have learnt to feed after sunset, catching the moths and other insects attracted by street lamps and the floodlighting of famous churches and other public buildings.

Apart from the nesting sites which man unintentionally provides in his houses and other buildings, he also sometimes deliberately provides nesting places for birds. This practice probably started for utilitarian reasons. Dovecotes supplied nesting and roosting places for semi-domesticated pigeons (probably their prototypes were first put

A male Lesser Kestrel at the entrance to its nest site in the walls of an old Abbey in southern France. This handsome little falcon now relies largely on man for its nesting places. (*C. C. Doncaster*)

up for wild Rock Pigeons that had begun to nest about houses) from which the young could be readily collected, for food or the droppings for fertiliser (or both). In many parts of Europe nest boxes were put up for Starlings and House Sparrows, whose young were likewise taken for food or, in the case of Sparrows to control their numbers. In northern Europe nest boxes were put up for Goldeneyes and other tree-nesting ducks, in order that their eggs might be collected more readily.

It is possible that in the case of pigeons, as with the White Stork previously discussed, nesting sites may sometimes have been provided for religious reasons. Pigeons (or doves – it is unfortunate that the English language has two names, with different emotional overtones, for birds of the same family) were sacred to Aphrodite in ancient Greece and have retained or acquired tinges of sanctity here and there in later human cultures as well as, perhaps, in earlier ones. A recent utilitarian use of artificial nest sites is for Hill Mynas in parts of Assam, where the young birds are taken, hand-reared and sold to the pet trade.

Increasingly in the past seventy years or so, man-made nesting places have been provided for aesthetic, humanitarian and scientific motives, as well as for new ways of putting birds to practical use. In Europe and North America nest boxes for various small insectivorous birds are put up in very large numbers, sometimes for aesthetic or sentimental reasons, sometimes to maintain or (hopefully) increase the numbers of species believed to control the numbers of insects harmful to forestry or other interests, sometimes to facilitate study of their biology and behaviour, and often from a mixture of two or more of these motives. With the exception of the American Purple Martin houses mentioned earlier, the majority of nest boxes put up were kinds suitable for species such as tits and the Starling or (different type) for the Robin and Spotted Flycatcher. Recently, however, many people and organisations have extended their scope in this matter, and nest boxes and baskets suitable for many other species, from the Treecreeper to the Tawny Owl, are locally in regular use.

The provision of artificial nesting sites is sometimes of great benefit to the birds concerned. Tits may be thereby enabled to breed in woodlands with few or no natural tree holes; the numbers of breeding Pied or Collared Flycatchers are sometimes dramatically increased when nest boxes are supplied; the provision of racoon-proof boxes, placed so that the ducklings will not have a long dangerous walk overland to the nearest suitable water, seems to have been a significant factor in the welcome increase of the beautiful Wood Duck in parts of North America. Taking a general view of the picture, however, even in such countries as western Europe, Britain and the U.S.A. it is likely that man's provision of nesting boxes has at best locally compensated for his destruction of natural sites. Modern forestry frowns on dead or dying trees, removes them, and even paints over the wounds of live trees so that holes will not develop in them. Similar actions, with less justification, are undertaken by some tidy-minded people in charge of parks and gardens. A picturesque dead tree in one public garden, that was no danger to anyone and much used by birds, was removed because it was claimed it would be offensive to the eyes of a visiting potentate. Ironically he is, in fact, a keen bird-watcher and most unlikely to have wished the tree removed. It is probable that the only species that may have been able to increase their populations, as distinct from having been able locally to maintain them at or near former levels, because of the provision of nest boxes, are those that benefit in other ways by man's activities, such as the Starling and the Great Tit.

Indeed it is possible that provision of nest boxes may have been detrimental to birds such as woodpeckers that excavate their own nest holes, by increasing the numbers of 'hole finders', such as the Starling, that often rob them of their newly-made nest sites.

Dogs, cats, and cattle

From very early times man has kept large numbers of domestic mammals; first the dog and later, but still for a long time, cattle, horses, sheep, goats, camels and what Shakespeare called 'the harmless, necessary cat'. I have already spoken of some of the ways in which some of these mammals help to alter the environment. Also of course, much of man's alteration of the land is or was concerned with his animal-keeping: maintaining pasture land, growing grain for pigs and chickens, killing wild animals to feed his dogs, and so on. Here I shall deal with a few of the more direct effects of man's domestic mammals on bird life.

As anyone will know who has ever walked in a field or along a woodland path in summer, any large creature disturbs grasshoppers and other insects as it moves about. A grazing cow or horse biting and tugging at the grass as it goes along, disturbs even more of them than we do. Several birds, in different parts of the world, habitually seek food around large grazing mammals, and catch insects disturbed by them. Over much of the world man has killed off most of the large grazing mammals such as wild cattle, bison and buffalo. Where he has not killed them all off he has usually reduced their numbers and restricted their range. Often, however, so far as the birds are concerned, his domestic cattle have filled the gap. Indeed, as domestic cattle are usually present in greater numbers and do not migrate large distances, they have probably often been much more convenient for certain birds than the wild herds they have replaced.

Earlier in this chapter I discussed the Cowbird of North America and mentioned the British Starling and Yellow Wagtail as species that habitually feed among grazing cattle. This habit is still more strongly developed in the Cattle Egret. This is a rather squat-looking little heron, about as big as a Rook. It is white, with pinkish-buff plumes on its head and back in the breeding season, from which it gets its alternative name of Buff-backed Heron.

Unlike most herons it does not usually feed in or near water but in fields and other open and quite dry places. Here it accompanies domestic cattle, stalking around them, catching the grasshoppers and other insects they disturb. When the particular cow that a Cattle Egret is feeding by moves quickly to another part of the pasture the bird will often trot after it with a comical-looking shambling gait. It perches on the backs of cattle and sometimes picks flies and ticks off them, although most of its food consists of grasshoppers and other insects that the cattle disturb.

When it has seen potential prey the Cattle Egret stalks it, takes

Cattle Egret and Ankole Cow. This small white heron habitually accompanies grazing mammals, to catch and eat the insects they disturb. It has thriven and spread as a result of man's cattle keeping and forest destruction. (*Eric Hosking*)

aim with an odd little waggle of its head that always reminds me of a golfer addressing the ball, and then catches it (or tries to catch it) with a quick lunge. Allowing for some minor differences, the movements are much the same as those of any other heron when catching prey. I did, however, once see a Cattle Egret behave in a remarkable way. It was in Egypt (during the Second World War) and a rather miserable-looking water buffalo was lying down on the bare, sun-baked earth outside its owner's mud-walled house. A Cattle Egret was standing by its head and, when I focused my glasses on it, I saw that it was eating the flies that clustered thickly at the corners of the buffalo's eyes. It caught the flies in the usual way except that, instead of stabbing fiercely forward to seize them, it picked them very gently, obviously not causing the least discomfort to the buffalo. I should like to know whether this Cattle Egret had learnt by experience that, if it was to feed from buffaloes' eyes, it must be 'gentle' or whether, perhaps, small, clustered insects are instinctively taken in this way.

This Cattle Egret, incidentally, was quite alone and I often saw lone individuals seeking food, although more often the species feeds in small or large flocks. In Egypt, where cattle are not very extensively kept, the Cattle Egret also feeds around men working in the fields, snatching the insects turned up with spade or hoe. It is, by the way, the bird that the dragoman usually points out to tourists as the 'Sacred Ibis', although the real Sacred Ibis is not now found in lower Egypt as it was, presumably, in the time of the Pharaohs.

The Cattle Egret's population, like man's, has been 'exploding' in the last fifty years or so. Previously it was only known to occur in Africa, Asia and south-western Europe. Now, however, it has, without so far as we know 'getting a lift' from man, colonised both North and South America and northern Australia. Its association with cattle has clearly been of importance in enabling it to succeed in this. Probably if any Cattle Egrets got to the New World or Australia before the invasion of these areas by Europeans and Asians and their cattle, they did not succeed in establishing themselves, as did the later arrivals.

Many people who like birds dislike cats. I am not one of them. Cats can, however, be an intolerable nuisance at times if one has an outdoor aviary, or if one is trying to study birds in a town or suburban garden. The domestic cat, like its wild ancestor, is preeminently a hunter of small mammals such as mice and voles. In country places where these are abundant it does not usually catch many birds. Even in the country some individual cats do, however, specialise in catching birds and a few even in finding and climbing to birds' nests, but on the whole cats do not catch as many birds as some people think they do.

In towns, where there are few or no small mammals, cats catch, in proportion to their numbers, very many more birds than they do in the country. They may even prevent some species, especially those that normally nest near the ground or on the ground itself, from being as numerous as they might otherwise be. Where cats are very plentiful, as in parts of suburban London, England, they also often prevent birds from feeding in gardens by habitually hunting and frightening them.

Dogs are not often thought of as harmful to birds, but at least in England they probably have a more significant effect on bird-life than cats do. They certainly do not *catch* many birds and some people who would hate to see a cat catch *one* Skylark are amused when their dog dashes madly about a field, hunting up dozens of Skylarks and chasing excitedly below them as they fly off. If the field is large and the dogs few no harm may be done, but in open spaces near towns and suburbs the amount of disturbance is considerable. If dogs are chasing all over a field in which there is a Skylark's or Meadow pipit's nest the birds will not be able to return to cover their eggs or feed their young until after the dogs have gone. If it is a Sunday there may be dogs there all day and the young birds will starve. Similarly, if a dog finds a hen Pheasant with small chicks she will probably succeed in deflecting its attention from her young while they scatter and hide. If, however, more and more dogs come to rampage around the area she may not become sufficiently at ease to call the chicks together again to brood them before they have become too numbed by cold to respond to her call, and so they will die.

I think, in fact, that domestic dogs, not the few that have gone feral and are hunting and scavenging to get their living (these are now rare in Britain) but the household pets that are brought usually by car to the nearest 'nice open space' for exercise, are an important factor in keeping the numbers of such ground-nesting birds as Skylarks, Meadow and Tree Pipits, Pheasants, and Partridges lower than they would otherwise be in some places, and in wholly preventing them from breeding in others. This is, however, an opinion not a proved fact. It would be most interesting to try to find two comparable open areas *which were equally subject (or not subject) to other forms of disturbances by man*, one of which was often overrun by numbers of dogs and the other not, and note to what extent the bird-life of the two differed.

In countries where dogs are common town and village scavengers they are serious competitors for food with vultures, kites and crows. Also, it is highly likely that much of the bread now consumed by sparrows and pigeons in London, England, would be eaten first by dogs (especially the large crusts that are often thrown down) if London now had the large, free-ranging and hungry feral dog population that characterised it ninety years or so ago, and which has long since been replaced by a population of well-fed pet dogs, only a few of whom are allowed to roam the streets, unaccompanied by their owners.

CHAPTER TWO

BIRDS IN TOWNS

Many people think of 'wild' country, particularly woods and forests, as full of birds and they often tend to talk as though towns and cities were birdless or nearly so. In fact, there are usually plenty of birds in towns even though not as many species may be represented as in the surrounding countryside. Travellers often complain with some truth that towns are becoming more and more alike the world over, but there are still some differences between towns, even in the same country, and far more between those in different countries. These differences are reflected in their bird life. For example, a town that has many parks or open spaces with ponds and lakes may have ducks, coots and other water birds which will obviously be absent in an otherwise similar town that has no such sheets of water. A large town with much atmospheric pollution is likely to harbour little insect life and so cannot support such purely insectivorous birds as swallows, except perhaps on its periphery. A town surrounded by open agricultural country may be used for nesting by species that feed in open fields, and which could not so use a town surrounded by a large suburban area.

Whatever sort of town they inhabit, however, town birds have to live in close proximity to large numbers of people. How these people feel about birds is of the utmost importance to their continued existence. Unless the townspeople are friendly, or at least not actively hostile towards it, a bird has little chance of establishing or maintaining itself among them. This does not mean that a species cannot succeed in town unless *everybody* refrains from persecuting it, merely that, on balance, human reactions to it must be favourable or neutral. In many towns in Britain, Europe and America, for example, thousands of Feral Pigeons are destroyed periodically by public officials at the taxpayers' expense. As, however, the majority of the townspeople like to see the pigeons, and continue to feed them, such mass killings have no lasting effect. New pairs soon begin to breed in the vacant nest sites and the population rises within a few months to its former levels. Were everyone to persecute or even to cease to feed the pigeons, then, at least in those towns where they rely mostly on public feeding, their numbers would soon greatly diminish.

At one time the Raven and the Kite were abundant and tolerated scavengers in London, England, but, as any reader of Shakespeare will know, they inspired little kindly feeling. I think they probably declined and finally vanished from London not only because of changed human feeding habits (less meat and fish and more farinaceous foods) of the Londoners and their (allegedly) less uncleanly methods of disposing of waste foodstuffs, but also because public feeling was against rather than in favour of them. Reading Oliver Goldsmith's descriptions, in his *History of the Earth and Animated Nature*, written in the eighteenth century, of the hideous cruelties inflicted on nestling Kites by 'the boys with their usual appetite for mischief' one does not get the impression that either he or his contemporaries thought this particular 'mischief' especially reprehensible. As an habitual predator on young domestic poultry the Kite was always hated by those who kept chickens. Now that it has been reduced (in Britain) to a pitiful remnant it is no longer a byword for abuse but receives the adulation reserved for rarities. To read some of the panegyrics now written about it would, indeed, lead anyone who did not know the bird to imagine, quite wrongly, that it is more beautiful and less capable of annoying anybody than the gulls and pigeons that scavenge in modern London.

No bird species can have originated in towns. Equally, most towns started as villages or at any rate as very much smaller towns than they are today. In many cases birds already living in and around villages managed to adapt, over the generations, as the village became a town. Some, like London's Feral Pigeons, increased in numbers as the town increased its size and density, while others finally failed to breed successfully when the town became too big, as did London's Rooks, and more recently, its Jackdaws and most of its House Martins.

I propose to discuss some of the characteristic birds of some towns that I know or have visited, how they get their living and the type of *original* habitat they are naturally adapted to. As it is likely that in some cases changes in the bird-life may have taken place since I was there, I will put in brackets the year or years of my observations.

London, England (1936–1940, 1946–1976)

London is a good place to watch birds. Even inner London has a large number of species and, if those responsible for its parks and public gardens were less obsessed with the urge to 'tidy up' any dense ground cover or dead trees, it would certainly support even more species, and some that are now rare or transient would become more common. The tiny Holland Park, whose administrators are, by and large, an exception to the above stricture, shows what can be done in allowing conditions suitable for a variety of birds without in any way curtailing the enjoyment of the visitors, indeed much increasing it.

The House Sparrow is often spoken of as the typical bird of London. It is certainly one of the most numerous and, like the Feral Pigeon, is seen even in the most densely built-up areas. The House Sparrow probably evolved somewhere in northern Africa or the Middle East. It was originally a bird of arid regions with thorn scrub or similar bushy cover and, like other species of sparrows, fed largely on seeds, especially the seeds of grasses. Quite possibly some of the grasses ancestral to our cultivated cereals were among its original food plants. At any rate it early attached itself to agricultural man and followed him to Britain, among other places. Primarily attached to man in the role of grain thief, and still the dominant bird of farmsteads and villages, it has everywhere successfully invaded large towns as well. In London, it fed at one time largely on grain spilled from horses' nosebags, but now its mainstay, except around docks and warehouses where grain is stored or loaded (and spilt), is bread and other food given to it or thrown away by people. It also takes the seeds of many wild and cultivated plants especially those of the Annual Meadow Grass (this ill-named grass is rare in meadows but grows commonly at roadsides and on flower beds in London) and the Common Knot-grass. It feeds its young nestlings mostly on insects. At least it tries to do so but in town these are in short supply and although the London Sparrow, when it has young to feed, seeks insects with a despairing versatility, fluttering and clambering up tree trunks to pick them from the bark, hovering over and plunging down after them into long grass, and investigating the undersides of the overhanging parts of iron rails and fences for insects resting there, as well as picking them from the leaves or ground in a more usual manner, it very often fails to get sufficient. Hence many young Sparrows in London and other large towns leave their nests in poor condition and still unable to fly properly.

Such weakly youngsters are particularly likely to fall victims to the domestic cat. Other predators on the House Sparrow in London are the Kestrel (House Sparrows are the main food of inner London's Kestrels), the Tawny Owl, which takes them at night from their roost, and the Jay which, ignoring the chattering alarm notes of the parents, tears open such House Sparrows' nests as it can find and reach and eats or carries off the eggs or nestlings. These predators are, however, too few even to prevent many sickly House Sparrows from surviving a long time, let alone to make any significant difference to the species' numbers.

Bold and impudent though it seems and capable of becoming hand tame when necessity demands, as in some of the London parks where in winter this tameness is of vital importance in enabling it to compete for handouts with the gulls and pigeons, the House Sparrow usually tends to be wary and mistrustful rather than otherwise. Even in places where man has hitherto tolerated it, if people take action against it with guns or traps, it learns much more quickly than most other birds do, who and what is dangerous and how to evade the danger. At least the survivors do and there are usually plenty of them.

The Starling can be seen feeding in most of London's parks and squares although by day it is far more abundant in suburban gardens and more or less open pastoral country. At night, however, it probably outnumbers all other species in the metropolis. Its roosts in the park trees or on the buildings around and near Trafalgar Square are one of the sights of the town. This habit of roosting in towns is now common in most countries where the Starling is found, and in cities as far apart as New York and Melbourne the birds' pre-roosting communal singing often bids fair to drown the sound of the congested traffic in the streets below them. Some people think that

Starlings roosting on ledges of the Admiralty Arch, Trafalgar Square, London. Starlings roost communally in many towns; most of the birds involved feed by day in the surrounding suburbs or countryside. (*Eric Hosking*)

Starlings only roost in inner London during the autumn and winter. This is not so but it is about mid-autumn, when their arrival into town coincides with the nightly exodus of office workers, that they are often first noticed. Also in late spring and summer a majority (but by no means all of them) roost in trees in the parks, especially St James's Park, changing over to the buildings after the leaves have fallen. Most of the Starlings that roost in London feed by day in the suburbs within a radius of about 25 kilometres or less of their roosts. From ringing returns it appears that most of the Continental Starlings that winter in Britain sleep at country roosts in woods or reedbeds.

In spite of its success at roosting in inner London the Starling is not such a strikingly successful species there by day as it is in suburbia. Numerous individuals do, however, seek insect food on the grass in the parks and compete with the other birds, not too successfully, for handouts from the public.

Three species of typical thrushes are common in London but only one of them, the Blackbird, is an outstanding success. There is hardly a lawn or garden plot, however small, that does not have at least a pair of Blackbirds regularly foraging on it in search of earthworms. They also eat many kinds of insects and fruit, and readily take bread and other artificial foods. The Blackbird is very successful in driving other birds, including the other thrushes, from food in field or garden, but has little luck when competing with a hurly-burly of gulls, ducks or pigeons in town parks. Like other thrushes it has the habit, when it finds a large and possibly edible object that is not trying to escape or at least not making any effective-looking movements to that end, of pausing and contemplating it for a moment before pouncing and seizing it. This probably serves under more natural conditions to let the bird take good aim and also to prevent it from too hastily grabbing a possibly dangerous prey. It is, however, fatal to success when the object is a piece of bread or cake and there are a dozen hungry birds within reach of it that do not have this habit. I have, however, on three occasions seen a Blackbird (not the same one) successfully compete with gulls and pigeons by what *appeared* to be a deliberate and cunning stratagem. In each case the Blackbird came flying out of cover when food was thrown. A crowd of Feral Pigeons and, in one instance, also many Black-headed Gulls, were already all round the food when the Blackbird alighted near them and at once gave a loud chattering scream. The pigeons and gulls reacted by flying off in a momentary panic. The Blackbird looked around apprehensively then, before they had come back, hopped to the food and either ate some or flew off with a large piece. This appears to be deliberate cunning but I do not think it really was. This chattering scream is given in sudden alarm, but it also seems to be uttered sometimes by a Blackbird suddenly excited for some other reason. I think in all these instances the call was given as an expression of frustration or annoyance because the food was out of reach, but the other birds mistook its significance and after they had flown up in alarm the Blackbird, having looked around for any danger (being itself alarmed by the others flying up) and seen none, noticed the food now once more available to it. It would be interesting to know whether a Blackbird ever learns from such experiences deliberately to give such a call in such a situation.

The Blackbird is naturally a bird of woodland and wood edge but in England, and many other parts of Europe, it long ago took to living also in gardens and parks. Where these have an abundance of fairly thick bushes, interspersed with lawns and fruit trees, they seem to suit the Blackbird's requirements even better than does its natural environment, especially if man supplies artificial food in hard weather. Such places as, for example, Kew Gardens and the Oxford Botanical Garden support a much higher density of Blackbirds than does natural woodland. The Blackbird has come into towns via parks and gardens and is still very largely dependent on the natural food it can find in them. It will, however, often visit window ledges and backyards in completely built-up areas, although seldom more than a stone's throw from a park or garden. On one occasion some years ago, at the entrance of Charing Cross station, I was surprised to see rubbish and pigeon droppings falling in quantity on to the pavement. Looking up, I saw that the culprit was a cock Blackbird. Some advertisement hoardings had been removed, exposing the droppings and old nests of generations of Feral Pigeons that had bred and roosted on the ledge behind and sheltered by the hoardings. The Blackbird was searching there, probably for the larvæ of the various beetles that breed in such places, digging into the mass and throwing it to right and left just as he would have done among the dead leaves of a wood.

The Blackbird builds its nests in bushes or trees. In a truly wild environment it usually nests low down in fairly thick cover, but in parks and gardens the choice is often not so wide and because there are usually fewer predators, there are more chances of conspicuous nests being successful. Town Blackbirds often nest about buildings, on ledges, in ventilation spaces and similar places. This does not really represent any great change in behaviour. When seeking a nest site the Blackbird, like many (but not all) bush and tree-nesting species, likes some fairly firm support, either of a largish branch or a fork, with cover around or above it. Often this cover will give additional support or serve as attachment for the sides of the nest. For species that choose this sort of site a great many rather different situations in different sorts of trees or bushes are all quite suitable. Such species, once they become used to perching on buildings and feel quite at ease there, are quite ready to nest there too if they find a site that fills their idea of suitability. The same is true of many other tree-nesting birds – such as some pigeons and jays for example – when they live in towns or villages. On the other hand birds that build more specialised nests in more specialised sites, such as the many tropical and subtropical species that attach their nests to the ends of slender branches, are unable to find nesting sites on buildings.

Young Blackbirds leave their nests when they are still not able to fly fully, but only to flutter a little distance. They then hide, each by itself, in the vegetation for some days before they begin to show themselves and to follow their parents. This behaviour, which is shown by many species that have open nests in bushes or scrub, serves to lessen the chances of all the brood being destroyed should a predator find the nest. The lone nestling hidden in the bushes is, at worst, in no greater risk of being discovered than it would be if it remained in the nest till it could fly fairly well. This, however, is only true in a more or less natural environment. If the nest is in a tidy town park or on a building with paved streets below, the fledgling is very liable to come to grief when it leaves the nest or very soon after. Every spring one hears anguished accounts from London bird-lovers of 'their' young Blackbirds having been run over, carried off by cats or dogs, or 'vanishing' when they left the nest. Sad as these tragedies of the individual are the species is certainly in no present danger. Everything suggests that enough young Blackbirds are reared in London to fill the gaps left by the deaths of adults. Even if there were not it is fairly certain that plenty of new recruits seeking a place to live in an overcrowded world would come in from the surrounding suburbs and countryside.

I am not sure that the Carrion Crow ought really to be included here but it is a favourite bird of mine. Although not as numerous as some species that I am leaving out it is abundant and conspicuous.

Most of the larger squares have a nesting pair of Carrion Crows. The larger open spaces on the periphery hold many more and there is a big communal roost in Ken Wood, on Hampstead Heath, to which Carrion Crows come each evening from all over London. The Carrion Crow is the only 'black' crow which still manages to thrive in the metropolis and that with little deliberate help from the public and active persecution from the officials in charge of some parks.

The Carrion Crow inhabits many different types of country, from wild moorland and upland pastures with only a few scattered and wind-bitten trees to open woodlands and parks. It seeks its food on the ground and takes many kinds of animal and vegetable food. Unfortunately for itself this includes, at times, the eggs and young of game-birds, so it is ruthlessly persecuted in many country districts. It is also accused of killing or blinding weakly lambs, but from what I have seen and from what I have heard from first-hand observers I think it is often blamed unjustly through being found feeding on lambs which have already died or been killed by foxes or dogs. A great deal of the Carrion Crow's food consists of insects; it spends much of its time searching for these in grassland and seems to eat many of small size that one would hardly think worth the searching for by so large a bird. In the heyday of gamekeeping in the latter part of the last and the early years of this century the Carrion Crow was so intensively shot and trapped that it became quite rare in many places. This is presumably the reason for the statement, often given in bird books of that period, that the Carrion Crow is a solitary bird. In fact even breeding pairs frequently gather with their neighbours and indulge in self-assertive displays on or near their territorial boundaries. Non-breeding birds associate in loose parties, and large numbers gather at communal roosts at all times of year.

Although the Carrion Crow because of its fear of man, caused by its long history of persecution in the country and the more local and sporadic persecution in London, does not usually profit directly from man's bounty in inner London, it does take a considerable amount of bread and other human food. The crust too hard for the House Sparrows and pigeons to break up, at which they are vainly pecking, is often carried off by a Carrion Crow as soon as it sees that the coast is clear. Locally some Carrion Crows have even learned that some individual human beings bear them no ill will and they will approach these individuals, but *not* other people, and take the food thrown to them. I once came on a man on Hampstead Heath, surrounded by numbers of crows, which he was feeding, but as soon as I appeared, forty metres away, off they all flew. Their benefactor seemed to share their feelings, as he cast one look at me and then hurried away; making me feel doubly guilty at my intrusion. The Crow also takes lumps of bread and bones that have been dropped, usually by gulls, on roof tops, and forages along the river's edge at low tide for edible flotsam and jetsam such as young or sick pigeons that have fallen from their nests or roosting places under the bridges, drowned and later been washed ashore.

Like the House Sparrows, London Carrion Crows often seem to have difficulty in finding sufficient food, in terms of quality rather than quantity, for their young. Many of the young Carrion Crows that one sees trailing after their parents in June and July are rather poor specimens. Often they have white bands or patches on their wings. This partial albinism is usually due to a deficient diet during the nestling period and, if the young Crows survive to their first complete moult, they become all black like their parents. Incidentally, the common idea that, because they scavenge on garbage tips and similar places, Carrion Crows will thrive on anything edible and are easy to keep is far from true. Birds of the crow family need plenty of space for exercise and a varied and fairly vitamin-rich diet if they are to thrive in captivity. So far as British species go this is particularly true of the Carrion and Hooded Crows and the Rook, as is often all too evident from the poor condition of some of these birds in some zoos and public aviaries.

In most large towns in England, and in many other parts of the world also, the Feral Pigeon is one of the commonest birds. In the very densely built-up parts of London it is the most abundant species, not excepting even the House Sparrow. In the less man-congested areas it is not quite so numerous, although it is common even in the outer suburbs. Feral Pigeons are descended from Domestic Pigeons, all of which were derived from the wild Rock Pigeon or Rock Dove.

Rock Pigeon in a snow-covered Shetland field. The Rock Pigeon probably only spread north from Mediterranean regions in the wake of agricultural man. This species is the ancestor of our domestic pigeons and their feral descendants that so brighten our grimy towns. (*Bobby Tulloch*)

This is a very handsome pigeon with light bluish-grey wings, crossed by two conspicuous black bars, a glossy green and purple neck, white lower back and white underwing coverts. Plenty of Feral Pigeons are of this colour pattern, which pigeon fanciers term 'blue' or 'blue barred', although 'blue chequers' – that is, birds that have the wing bars broader and all the wing coverts spotted with black, to varying degrees – are usually even more abundant and 'dark chequers' – with the wing coverts mainly blackish – are just as common. In London and many other places Feral Pigeons show a great variety of colour patterns and besides the 'blue black' colour patterns, one finds 'dominant reds' (similar to the blue colours but with reddish-brown markings on a creamy-grey ground instead of black on bluish grey, and with no dark bar on the tail); 'grizzles' (which can be any colour and are characterised by having an odd, streaky intermixture of white on all the feathers); 'recessive reds' (a deep reddish or pinkish brown with no markings, but often with blue-grey rump and tail); 'blacks' (entirely sooty or slaty black except for their neck gloss), and many other colours, all of which may also be 'pied' (with white, unpigmented areas of plumage).

Wild Rock Pigeons inhabit coastal or inland cliffs where they roost on sheltered ledges and nest on ledges in caves or in holes or crevices. In some places, usually in semi-desert or desert regions, they also live in potholes, sometimes nesting and roosting far underground. They feed on seeds and, to a lesser extent, small snails, buds and other food that they find in open country where the plant cover is either sparse or very short. In some towns and in many suburbs Feral Pigeons obtain part or all of their food in the same way, but in London and most other large towns the majority of them feed in the streets and parks, usually only a short distance from their roosting sites. In such places they get relatively little food other than what is given to them or thrown away by people. Therefore bread and similar foodstuffs bulk largely in their diet, although they usually prefer grain or peanuts, and also take meat, fat, cheese, chocolate and many other foods. The recognition of such unnatural foods as bread and meat seems to be largely acquired through trial and error and by seeing other pigeons eat it. The Rock Pigeon's bill and its feeding movements evolved for picking up seeds and swallowing them whole, so it is not surprising that it has difficulty with some of the man-made foodstuffs. A Pigeon feeding on a large lump of bread picks it up, shakes it and flings it about. Sometimes a slice of bread gets its soft centre eaten first and then is accidentally flung back over the bird's own head, lands on its neck, slips below the feathers and may be held there for some hours in spite of the bird's effort to free itself! The movements that the Feral Pigeon uses to try to break bits off a large lump of bread or meat consist of seizing a morsel in the bill, pulling, and then violently shaking the head, or seizing a morsel and then making a shaking movement without lifting the head, so that the object held in the bill tip is rubbed on the ground. These are all movements which are used under natural conditions, respectively, to pluck seeds from the ears of grasses, sedges or other plants and to remove 'winged' seeds, such as those of Wych Elm, from their attachments. With some nearly ripe seeds they are highly efficient, but they are less so with bread, unless it is very soft, while with a lump of meat or suet town Pigeons, usually desperately hungry for fat and protein, often get their plumage in a terrible mess and succeed in detaching and swallowing very little before some gull, Mallard or Carrion Crow takes the booty from them.

It is not only such obvious sources as the large parks and squares with their many lunch-time visitors that provide feeding places for Pigeons. Every coffee stall or open-air snack bar where the careless may drop or the kindly throw a bit of bun or sausage roll; the side door of the big restaurant where the transfer of large numbers of loaves from the van that brings them results in many crumbs falling on road or pavement; the sheltered steps and archways where the ragged human derelicts, themselves hunched miserably like starved Pigeons, consume and often share their meagre scraps; all these have been discovered and are regularly taken advantage of by at least a few Feral Pigeons.

Feral Pigeons nest, when they can, on well-sheltered ledges or in holes in buildings, equivalents of their ancestors' cave or cliff sites. Good nesting sites are, however, in short supply in London and are becoming ever scarcer, with the continual pulling down of old buildings and dwelling houses and their replacement by cubical skyscraping office blocks. In inner London I have never seen a site that looked suitable for a Pigeons' nest that was not already in use. Many pairs can find nowhere to nest in spite of their constant searching. As yet, however, shortage of nest sites seems not sufficiently acute to have any effect on the Pigeon's numbers. There appear to be more than enough breeding pairs to keep numbers up to the limit imposed by the food supply. Every one of the older bridges over London's Thames, for example, provides nest sites for scores, often hundreds of pairs.

London's Feral Pigeons have few natural enemies. In or near the parks some Tawny Owls take young from nests and sometimes also roosting adults. The Carrion Crow robs such nests as it can reach without venturing too deeply between or inside buildings, and cats occasionally catch both young and adults on the ground. None of these predators takes any appreciable toll of the population. Official man, in strong contrast to and often much against the wishes of non-official man, is an enemy who locally and periodically kills large numbers of Feral Pigeons. The black cotton put over crocuses to keep off the Sparrows and pieces of thread and wool thrown down by women in the parks and gardens and the bits of discarded fishing line by lakes and (in outer London) riverside are apt to get tangled round Pigeons' feet, pull tight and ultimately result in mortification and loss of toes or even the whole foot. Probably many individuals die as a result of such crippling. Some, however, survive. A hen Pigeon who had lost both feet lived in and around St James's Park for at least eighteen months, toddling awkwardly on her stumps. When I first saw her these had already healed. How she had got about sufficiently to feed in the early stages of mortification I have no idea, but she evidently managed it somehow. Some Pigeons get run over and, as with human beings, it is the young and inexperienced, the sick, the aged, and the crippled who are the most frequent victims of the road hog.

Virgil wrote that one of the pleasures of living in the country was to hear the cooing of 'the hollow-voiced Wood Pigeon'. The modern Londoner can share this pleasure whether he lives in the city itself or in one of its ever-spreading suburbs. The Wood Pigeon was originally a bird of deciduous or mixed forests, probably most common in forests with many open glades. It feeds on a great variety of seeds, from those of various grasses and weeds to beechnuts and acorns, buds, young vegetation, berries and, to a lesser extent, such invertebrates as small snails, earthworms, and caterpillars. Unlike other British pigeons, which are mainly ground feeders, the Wood Pigeon also feeds much in the branches of trees and shrubs. When the last acorns or berries that it can reach by perching have been eaten it will hang upside down, usually with its wings spread against the twigs for added support, and in this position pluck and swallow those that it cannot otherwise reach.

The Wood Pigeon seems to have first attracted notice in London's larger parks in the latter part of the last century and to have become abundant and widespread by 1900. In the 1930s it was extremely common all over London and in inner London many of the Wood Pigeons were as tame as the tamest Feral Pigeons. During the Second World War London's Wood Pigeons were shot both for food and because of the damage they were capable of doing in the vegetable allotments that were then officially encouraged. When I returned to England in 1946 I found a very great contrast to the situation in 1939. The claim published in a newspaper in June 1941 and attributed to one or other of the ministries, that the Wood Pigeon would be exterminated, had not been fulfilled. There were still plenty of Wood Pigeons even in London. They were, however, much wilder than before the war. It was not until the summer of 1949 that I again saw a Wood Pigeon feeding from the hand and it was not until another year had passed that such tameness began to be once more quite common among them.

The Wood Pigeons of inner London compete with the Feral Pigeons for bread given by people. This is probably quite an important part of their diet, especially in late spring and summer when most of them are breeding. The two pigeon species do not, however, compete with one another for natural foods, the Wood Pigeon takes the buds and young leaves of hawthorn, lilac, black poplar, elm and other trees; berries of holly, ivy, rowan, hawthorn, mulberry, and some other trees and acorns. These foods are hardly eaten at all by most Feral Pigeons. Both the Wood Pigeon and the Feral Pigeon feed on the seed heads of Annual Meadow Grass and Rye Grass, but when the grass is seeding this food is so plentiful that they cannot be said to compete for it. Most London Wood Pigeons leave their nesting territories in early autumn and return to them some time between the end of October and March. During their absence they almost certainly form part of the large numbers that gather to feed on acorns or beechnuts in such places as Hampstead Heath and Richmond Park. Their going away does not, however, seem to be in search of food, as individuals with an assured food supply go like the rest. For six years I fed a hen Wood Pigeon that came to my window in South Kensington. She thus had a regular supply of food but every year, towards the end of every September, I would one day notice a change in her demeanour. She was not less tame towards me but she was 'jumpy' and 'on edge'. She would suddenly stop feeding, look around, and tremble for no obvious reason. (I say 'for no obvious reason' since at all times she would tremble in this manner if any other Wood Pigeon, except her mate, suddenly appeared.) After one to three days of this she would be gone and I would see her no more until one day she would be back on the windowsill waiting for handouts just as if she had never been absent. The first year I knew her (she was adult when she first came and was caught and ringed) she left in late September and returned in February, but in subsequent years she tended to return earlier and once, the fourth year of our acquaintance, she was back in late October.

This autumnal exodus represents a post-breeding migration from the breeding areas and it seems likely that the birds do not return until they are once more coming into breeding condition. London Wood Pigeons, or at any rate some of them, begin to display and show other sexual behaviour as early as November although few of them breed until March or even later. The annual autumnal period during which most of them are living independent of man's charity appears to eliminate all the physically defective individuals. Like the Feral Pigeons, London's Wood Pigeons produce some young with hook bills and other deformities, but whereas in the case of the former such individuals sometimes live, or at least drag out a rather miserable existence for some years, nearly all deformed young Wood Pigeons evidently die during their first autumn and winter when they are dependent on natural foods.

Wood Pigeons are common throughout the suburbs where they regularly feed in quite small gardens and at bird-tables. Where I now live, at Herne Hill in south London, the Feral Pigeons scavenge in the roads and the Wood Pigeons, which nest in the roadside trees, sometimes join them there. Both species feed in numbers on the open lawns surrounding the blocks of council flats where large amounts of bread and other food are thrown for them, but only Wood Pigeons habitually come down into the small gardens, like my own.

Being naturally woodland birds they are less unwilling to come to the ground in a small and more or less enclosed area. When so doing they are cautious and wary but not always wary enough, as some fall victims to domestic cats. On the whole, however, London's Wood Pigeons have few natural predators and, as only the odd pair or two nest on buildings, they are not usually persecuted. Indeed I once saw a touching and amusing instance of the average Londoner's fondness for birds exemplified with this species. Periodically 'Authority' sends round men with ladders and saws to 'prune' the roadside trees. This 'pruning' usually consists of removing most of the branches and leaving the trees, mere mutilated stumps. On one of the doomed branches, of a tree just by a bus stop, was a Wood Pigeons' nest which at the time had two young about a week old. The woodmen did not spare the tree but they spared the branch with the nest. They left it sticking out alone and fully exposed for all to see. But all went well. The parents continued to tend their offspring full in the public eye, no predator discovered the nest, and the young were successfully fledged.

The Wood Pigeon nests in trees and bushes, but in towns it will on occasion nest on a ledge of a building. It likes a fairly sheltered ledge when it does so, and in London such sites are usually already in the possession of Feral Pigeons. The Wood Pigeon is, however, often able to get a nest to 'stay put' in places where Feral Pigeons are usually unable to. For example, there was a row of pipes under a colonnade where for years Feral Pigeons had tried in vain to build. All the material they brought fell to the ground between the pipes. Then a pair of Wood Pigeons took over the site, built a nest on it and reared two young. They then (it being late September) left the area. While they were away a pair of Feral Pigeons took over their old nest. The Feral Pigeons held it successfully against all comers, including the returning Wood Pigeons, for several years, adding more and more material and rearing brood after brood, until the resultant pile of twigs and droppings was torn down by a Ministry of Works official. Being a tree-nester the Wood Pigeon can spread its breeding population more evenly over London than the Feral Pigeon. It is not true, however, as has been claimed by a well-known ornithologist, that 'every tree provides the Wood Pigeon with suitable nest sites'. Tree-nesting pigeons usually need some sort of more or less horizontal support to build on. Typical sites are where two or more nearly horizontal boughs come fairly close together, on a large bough that has upward-growing shoots at its sides that provide some additional support, on top of a cut- or broken-off stump with similar upward- or outward-growing shoots surrounding it, on or among the dense mass of twigs of a 'witches' broom' in a lime or other tree subject to this malady, or on top of the old nest of a Jay or some other bird.

London Wood Pigeons often have difficulty in finding a nest site within their territory. Sometimes, they eventually manage to use a site that seems at first impossible. For example, in the spring of 1963 a pair whose territory included part of the road where I live searched in the six or seven roadside trees available in their territory without finding a good place. Finally they began to 'call-to-nest' on a horizontal branch only a couple of centimetres in diameter and with, so far as I could see, no other branches near enough to be of use as supports. The male soon began to collect nesting material but every twig fell down. This went on for about five weeks. Every morning as I went to work, I saw the female crouching on her branch, often her mate arriving with a twig or in the act of passing it over to her, and a litter of twigs on the pavement below. Finally the birds gave up, but they came back again for a period in early August with equal lack of success. Early in 1964 they returned to the same site. This time, however, after they had been 'going through the motions' of nest-building for about three weeks, one or two extra long twigs which the male brought caught up on some living twigs only 30 centimetres away from the branch on which the hen crouched. Once these first twigs 'stayed put' others soon followed and within a week a nest had been constructed. The pair reared three broods on it that year, building a fresh nest on top of the old each time so that it became very bulky and looked very insecure, as indeed it was. The rains and winds of autumn and winter did it no good at all and when the pair returned to it in February 1965 it collapsed beneath their weight and fell out of the tree. I was then away from home for eight months so I do not know what happened in 1965, but when I returned in October there was no nest. In late March 1966 the pair were back at the same nest site and trying to build but at first all material fell down. Later that spring, however, they succeeded in building a nest on the old site. After this young were reared on this site for many years. Sometimes the nest fell down but the birds always succeeded in building another on the site. In March 1972 there was a very large nest, as it was two years since it had last fallen. Then, however, the nest branch was cut off. I suspect by or at the instigation of one of the motorists who use the street for a garage, and objected to pigeon droppings on his car.

A rather similar instance occurred with another pair in a tree just in front of my next-door neighbour, where the persistent efforts of a pair with no alternative site eventually resulted in a nest being built in a place which everyone with experience only of Wood Pigeons in the country, where each pair usually has better sites available, would have thought impossible.

Cairo (1941–1942, 1945, 1947)

In spite of all its drawbacks, wartime Cairo had much to recommend it to the birdwatcher as well as to the lover of antiquities. Most conspicuous and characteristic of its birds (although probably not the most numerous) was the Black Kite. This is a large, dark brown hawk with long wings, a rather slender body and long, slightly forked tail. When adult, the Egyptian form has a yellow bill as have most of the other African races of this species. The juvenile birds have pale tips to their feathers, which gives them an attractive spotted appearance. The Black Kite is less handsome than the larger and brighter-coloured Red Kite which was once such a common scavenger in English towns that it gave its name to the toy which also floated and soared on the wind.

The Black Kite is found widely throughout the temperate and tropical parts of the old world from western Europe to China and Australia. In many places it has become a regular scavenger about towns and villages, taking any scraps of meat or fish that it can snatch up and preying on young chickens and ducklings when it gets the chance to do so. Under more natural conditions the Black Kite inhabits fairly open country, with some trees, or open woodlands adjacent to lakes, rivers or open areas, but it avoids tropical forest. It feeds on insects, reptiles, small mammals and birds. It is, however, not at all certain that all the many creatures that the Black Kite has been seen eating, or in possession of, were caught by it. It certainly takes poultry chicks, insects and lizards, and picks up dead or dying fish, but it also habitually chases and harries any other bird that it sees carrying food. If it cannot or dare not rob some other bird-of-prey it will wait while the latter feeds and then scavenge anything edible that is left. An ornithologist who studied this species in a completely wild environment in north-eastern Tibet never saw it kill prey for itself. The Black Kite sometimes feeds on the carcasses of large mammals but not, I think, to anything like the extent that Kipling in his ever memorable *Jungle Books* suggested. It seems probable that Black Kites have to learn that large carcasses can be a source of food. Their usual role at a carcass is as 'snappers-up of unconsidered trifles', darting down to pick up a bit of meat or offal dropped by a vulture outside the main 'scrum'. Probably the sight of the true carcass-eaters tearing at the meat is what attracts them in the first place. Some individual Black Kites may come to carcasses and open them up but many will not. In Egypt I have seen dead dogs and cats lying on garbage heaps ignored by the many Black Kites which were searching these for food.

When actively seeking food the Black Kite flies fairly low over the streets and roof tops, looking down. When it sees a piece of meat or offal lying in a possible place, where there is room for it to manœuvre, it swoops down and snatches up the morsel in one foot as it passes low over the ground. Although it shows much less speed and agility than some other hawks, for example, a Sparrowhawk catching a bird, the Black Kite's swoop is very impressive. As it rises it brings forward its foot and looks at what it has got, which always seems a touchingly 'human' action. Small objects are eaten on the wing, the Kite soaring round or continuing its flight whilst pecking at the food in its foot. Larger booty is usually taken to some perch. The sight of a Black Kite swooping attracts others, and one carrying a sizeable piece of food is usually chased and harried by its fellows. Indeed I had the impression that most young town Black Kites, after their parents ceased to feed them, became for some time almost wholly dependent on what they could rob from other Black Kites (or from Kestrels and Hooded Crows) rather than on getting food 'first hand' for themselves.

It is said that in India the Black Kite will eat such vegetable foods as cooked rice and bread. I never saw this in Egypt although some

Black Kites at their nest. Shakespeare's 'Where the Kite builds look to lesser linen' is now more applicable to the Black Kite, which is still a common town and village scavenger in many countries and fond of incorporating discarded or 'stolen' human clothing in its nest. (*Eric Hosking*)

would eat bread or pastry that was soaked or covered in grease or butter. Nor were the Cairo Black Kites, nor the many that frequented the various Army camps elsewhere in Egypt, so bold as their Indian counterparts which will regularly snatch food from people's hands. Many a time I watched Black Kites hovering low overhead when we were taking our plates or mess tins of food from cookhouse to mess tent. They would look down hungrily, their talons spasmodically clenching and unclenching in eagerness but 'letting I dare not wait upon I would'. Only twice did I see a Black Kite actually strike at food held by a man. In each case the swoop came at a moment when the man's face was turned away from the food. In the first instance a soldier had just come out of the NAAFI at the Kasr el Nil barracks with an egg sandwich. He took a bite out of it and then, declaiming to his companion, he threw back his arm, egg sandwich and all, to emphasise his remark. At once a Black Kite swooped and took the 'proffered' sandwich so neatly that its owner did not realise what had happened until he was told. The other incident also had its element of comedy for the watcher, but not for the hungry Black Kite. A soldier going to the mess tent (in Maadi camp) stopped to fill his mug from a water jar. As his head was turned away from the plate held out in his left hand a Black Kite, which had been trying to pluck up courage for several minutes, swooped down. In his alarm as its wing brushed his head the man dropped his plate; probably he moved a fraction of a second too soon and put the Black Kite off a bit. At all events when it brought forward its foot to look at what it had seized it saw that it had got only a potato and dropped it in disgust. Because the Black Kite snatches up food with one foot it does not have to check its speed as does a bird that picks up food with its bill, such as a gull.

It seems likely that the Black Kite began its career as a hanger-on of man when he was still a nomadic or semi-nomadic hunter. What is rather surprising is that an essentially meat- or fish-eating scavenging bird can exist in such great numbers in towns and villages in parts of the world where most of the people are themselves under-fed rather than otherwise, where, in many cases they eat little animal food, and where there are also numerous feral dogs. These at times

compete with Black Kites for food. I often noticed that if a pariah
dog saw Black Kites swooping down it would usually at once run
to the spot in hope of booty.

When ants were swarming the Black Kites would soar around,
taking the flying ants on the wing, the little insect being snatched
in the foot and eaten bill to foot in the usual way. Apart from this
I never actually saw a Black Kite in Cairo, or anywhere else, take
living prey. However, I climbed to three different Black Kites' nests
and in each of them found the downy nestlings surrounded by
freshly-killed young domestic fowls from one to seven weeks old.
Whether this means that breeding Black Kites have an increased urge
to take living prey when they have young to feed or that only individuals that have learnt to include such prey in their diet come into
full breeding condition and successfully rear young, I do not know.
Possibly both factors operate and are complementary.

The Black Kite builds a bulky nest of sticks, lined with any softish
rubbish it can pick up. Old papers, old socks, army puttees, and a
handkerchief were in the nests I climbed to. Shakespeare's 'Where
the Kite builds look to lesser linen' is as applicable to the Black Kite
as to its larger relative. The nest is built in a tree or, less often, on
some ledge of a building. In Cairo nests were often on palms, where
the large leaves join the trunk, but also on other trees, including quite
small roadside trees, and there was an enormous nest on the girders
under the roof of Cairo main railway station.

In the winter of 1944/5 I was stationed at an army camp at
Maadi, near Cairo. Here I often amused myself by gathering such
scraps as I could and feeding the Black Kites and Hooded Crows.
The average Englishman has a sentimental feeling for small passerine
birds but this is counterbalanced by his dislike of hawks and crows.
Thus although Black Kites were common scavengers about the camp
they were highly suspicious and not without good reason. One,
however, learned very quickly to recognise me and became surprisingly tame. After I had fed it only twice I was walking back from
the dining hall to my tent along a route where others identically
dressed were constantly passing to and fro, and noticed a Black Kite
perched on a pole some distance away. I looked towards it and as

I did so it stared back at me intently for a few seconds and then, to my astonishment, flew straight at me and hovered overhead till I flung it the expected tit-bit. Thereafter this Black Kite accosted me regularly when I returned from meals; at first rather hesitant and nervous, it soon became bolder and would snatch up a piece of meat or cheese thrown only a metre or so away from me without hesitation. When it was flying elsewhere in the camp an upward look and a gesture of my hand would bring it down at once for the morsel it hoped would be forthcoming. The Black Kite did not recognise me only by such gestures, as was proved by its coming to me on several occasions when I had no food for it and was doing nothing to attract its attention.

One day, after I had been feeding 'my' Black Kite for about a month it met me as usual when I returned from lunch, but as it swooped for the food I threw it, one of my companions, to annoy me, threw his tin plate at it. He narrowly missed the Kite which dropped its meat in fear and beat hastily into the safety of the upper air. In the bird's eyes I was damned along with the culprit. Although it afterwards recognised and came to me as before it never again took food from the ground near to me. It would hang overhead, much higher above than formerly, and only swoop down for the food when I was several metres away.

Another common and conspicuous bird in Cairo was the Hooded Crow. This bird was formerly thought to be a full species, but is now considered to belong to the same species as the all-black Carrion Crow. In general the black Carrion Crows are found in the south-western and far-eastern parts of the bird's range whereas the Hooded Crows, birds with the body mostly grey and the head, tail and wings black, are found in most of Europe and western Asia. Where the two forms meet as they do, for example, in the highlands of Scotland, they interbreed and one can find both black, hooded and intermediate birds in the same population.

In Cairo, and indeed throughout the Nile Delta, the Hooded Crow is extremely abundant, in spite of the fact that it is there near the southern limit of its range and always appears to feel the heat of the Egyptian summer quite as badly as any English visitor. On hot summer days when Black Kites float about high in the sky the Hooded Crow spends much of its time standing in the shade beneath some large tree, panting with gaping beak and with its wings held so as to allow the air to circulate between them and its body. Only towards evening and in the early morning does it show the same liveliness as characterises it during cooler periods.

The general remarks made about the Carrion Crow (page 56) apply equally to the Hooded Crow. Although the Egyptian form of the species has probably been long adapted to a rather drier climate it is in no sense a bird of the desert. It ventures into army camps and villages on the desert edge and there its foraging range overlaps that of the Brown-necked or Desert Raven, but otherwise it keeps strictly to the well-watered and cultivated delta of the Nile and the Suez Canal. In Egypt the Crow is treated with greater tolerance by man than its British counterpart. As a result it can and does exploit its environment more fully than the London Crow, seeking food not only in large open spaces and on roof tops but also in quite small gardens and yards. Its behaviour suggests, however, that man's tolerance of it is limited. Like the Black Kites and the pariah dogs, if one stooped as if to pick up a stone a nearby Crow would flee at once. I was, and still am, surprised at the apparent insight this behaviour showed. In the dogs it was understandable, as doubtless most of them had been hit by many a stone. It is, however, very unlikely that more than a minute fraction of the Kites or Crows had ever been actually struck by a missile yet many of them clearly recognised the preliminary movements as hostile in intent.

Alertness and suspicion are keynotes of the Crow's character and have been of the utmost value to it in its endeavour to live alongside man. I often noticed that if, when I passed near a Hooded Crow, I let a piece of bread or meat fall, as though by accident, the bird would hop up and take it before I had gone many metres. If, however, I looked at the Crow and then deliberately threw the food towards it the bird would at once take fright, fly off and perch at a distance. Only when I had gone a considerable way off would it come back, approach the food with care and much hesitation and, usually after having first pecked once or twice at it and jumped away in almost the same movement, seize the morsel and fly off with it. Here, incidentally, we see that a behaviour pattern – jumping in, pecking and quickly retreating only to repeat the process – which is naturally employed when dealing with possibly dangerous prey, may be used towards such inert food as a piece of bread because the crow has mentally associated it with a potentially dangerous creature (man).

The House Sparrow of Egypt is a different race of the species and differs more in appearance from the English Sparrow than does the Egyptian Hooded Crow from its Scottish relative. It is smaller and more clearly marked and looks much more sleek and spruce. This latter feature is probably largely a matter of climate. English House Sparrows, I have noticed, sleek down their plumage in warm weather and their usual rather puffy or ruffled appearance (even leaving sick and poorly plumaged individuals aside) may be due to their having not adapted sufficiently to the cold and wet of the British climate to be *comfortable* in it. In Cairo, and still more in the various Army camps around its outer suburbs, the House Sparrow was as ubiquitous as in England but bolder and more 'impudent'. As is the case with the species in India, Egyptian Sparrows come freely *inside* houses to nest or pick up scraps, if they are not actively discouraged; and sometimes even when they are!

At one large Army camp near Cairo we were issued with lots of a very nasty kind of marmalade. It came in big tins, was an unpleasing yellow-green colour and had an equally unpleasing bitter taste. The House Sparrows, however, loved it. They entered the mess tent, flew down on to the table and, half a dozen or more at a time, perched on the rim of the open marmalade tin and gobbled down the bitter goo as fast as they could. As House Sparrows in England sometimes eat sugar it may have been the sugar content, such as it was, that appealed to them. On the other hand at this camp the Sparrows seemed to feed mainly on scraps of white bread and army biscuit, so perhaps the marmalade either supplied some missing element of their diet or else suggested to them some natural food that would have done so.

Feral Pigeons were abundant in parts of Cairo but they seemed, so far as I could see, to use the buildings only for roosting and nesting and to get their food outside the city. The pigeon that really was one of the most abundant birds of Cairo was the Laughing Dove or Palm Dove. This is a pretty little bird rather smaller than the migratory Turtle Dove which frequents Britain, with proportionately much shorter wings and longer tail. Although not as beautiful as the Turtle Dove it is a handsome bird, reddish brown and slate blue with wine-tinged head and neck. On the sides and front of the neck it has an area of bifurcated feathers with blackish bases and bright coppery tips that show as a broad, brightly-spotted band when it swells out its neck in cooing or in its rapid bobbing bowing display. Its outer tail feathers are tipped white like those of most 'turtledoves'.

The Laughing Dove appears to be naturally a bird of arid areas with thorn or other scrub growth and some source of water within easy reach. Here it feeds, so far as is known, chiefly on seeds picked up out of the dusty ground and nests in shrubs and small trees. However, although common enough in some such areas in the wilds it is now typically a bird of human habitations; seeking spilled millet in the dust and drinking from the water jars in African villages, picking the crumbs from beneath café tables, coming to the windows of skyscrapers in modern towns, or tripping over the trim lawns of the grandiose mansions enshrining modern potentates. Friends who have been on safari in the African bush have told me that they always knew they were near a village if they saw a Laughing Dove or heard its soft rising and falling 'Cǒo-cǒo-cǒocǒo-cǒo' that, to some ears, suggests gentle laughter. The Laughing Dove is evidently a bird that has come to town *via* the village where man's grain growing and, above all, his provision of reliable water supplies, created suitable living conditions for it.

In Cairo Laughing Doves were everywhere about the buildings and roadside trees, nesting both in trees and shrubs, in niches and on sheltered ledges of buildings. They fed commonly on lawns of houses and clubs with European-style gardens, taking seeds of Annual Meadow Grass or a species very like it, and presumably seeds of other kinds as well. I also frequently saw them picking about in the less busy streets and I suspect that some people put food for them on balconies and roof tops also. Watching Laughing Doves in Egypt

I realised for the first time how much seed lies about in the dust in dry countries and remains in good condition for long periods, not almost immediately beginning either to germinate or to rot as it often does in damper climates.

Unlike such species as the House Sparrow and the Carrion Crow, the Laughing Dove does not appear to possess any innate tendency to suspicion or readiness at once to become timid, should man show hostility to it. Rather it seems to succeed because its air of gentle trustfulness tends to disarm people and make them kindly disposed towards it. Even in Egypt, with its then (1941–7) widespread poverty, I only came across a few cases of people killing the Laughing Dove for food. It is easy to shoot or trap and its success as a town or village bird must always be subject to the goodwill or tolerance of the vast majority of its human neighbours. Happily, most people extend it this tolerance.

Colombo (1965)

Colombo, capital of Sri Lanka, is the only old-world tropical town in which I have set foot, although in the spring of 1941 I spent three frustrating days looking at Freetown, West Africa, from a troopship anchored in the estuary. I must confess too that I only spent one day in Colombo and most of that time was in and around the harbour and in the grounds of Colombo Zoo, a wonderful place for any visitor to see *wild* birds without trouble. Coming at dawn into Colombo harbour after a week on nearly bird-less seas was like a feast after a fast. As soon as the ship entered harbour sleek, glossy House Crows came aboard looking for scraps; crowds of Whiskered Terns fluttered and dipped close around the ship, scavenging scraps like gulls in England; big, beautiful Brahminy Kites glided and wheeled around, not venturing so close as the terns but ever ready to chase any tern that had seized a scrap too large to swallow. A view through binoculars showed other terns and Indian Black-headed Gulls further off over the water and on land innumerable crows and Feral Pigeons on the harbour buildings.

The House Crow is often despised as a scavenger and disliked as a nest robber, but to anyone who looks at it with an unbiased eye it truly is a splendid crow and deserves its scientific name, *splendens*. It is mid-way in size between a Jackdaw and a Carrion Crow but more slimly built than either. Its forehead and face are glossy black, surrounded by a grey nape and neck which shades to darker grey or black on its back and belly. The wings and tail are black with vivid blue, green and purple gloss. It varies geographically, House Crows from north-western India being a pale milky grey on the neck and breast, whereas those from the warmer and more humid parts of its range, such as Sri Lanka and Burma, are much darker.

The House Crows that came aboard our ship were rather nervous and suspicious and, finding no food, soon left it. When I went ashore I was, however, able for the first time in my life to look at nearby wild crows without their showing any fear or even noticing that my gaze was fixed upon them. There were crows on the roofs, crows in the streets, crows in the palm trees. Wherever people were eating, if it was only an ice cream or some sweetmeats, one, two or several House Crows were loitering hopefully around. During the very brief time available I did not actually see anyone give any food to a crow but it was clear from the birds' behaviour that they were used to food being either dropped or given to them.

The House Crow is mainly a bird of the lowlands, but in parts of India it has followed the railway lines and roads to towns and settlements high in the hills. It is found in all kinds of country from semi-desert to tropical rain forest but always in or around human settlements. Since it is now found only in association with man it is not certain what type of country it originally inhabited. Although it feeds on all sorts of scraps of waste or 'stolen' human food, it also takes insects, lizards, young birds, fruit and similar natural foods and it is difficult to see why it cannot, or at any rate does not, manage to live away from man. Its larger relative, the all-black but almost equally sleek and glossy Jungle Crow, which often competes with the House Crow for scraps and offal in towns and villages, is common enough in the wilds, as its name indicates. Possibly the original habitat of the House Crow was highly suitable for man when he came

House Crows and Jungle Crows scavenging in an Indian town. The House Crow only lives alongside man; the larger Jungle Crow, as its name suggests, is also found in the wilds. (*Eric Hosking*)

on the scene, and the reason why this crow is not now found away from man may be that no part of its original home is now *not* overrun by human beings!

Although tame to the point of 'impudence' where not molested, the House Crow is quick to recognise the danger if man turns against it. I have been told by an Indian acquaintance who shares neither my admiration nor his people's usual tolerance for the House Crow that, when attempting to kill off the crows that visited his garden, he soon found it most difficult to shoot any, even from a hide. Indeed the only creature that habitually gets the better of the House Crow is the Koel, a species of cuckoo which is parasitic on it.

The Brahminy Kite was the most spectacular bird about Colombo harbour. Most were adults whose handsome chestnut plumage, set off by black wing quills and white heads and breasts, makes them one of the most strikingly handsome hawks in the world. The immature birds in their streaky warm brown dress look dull by comparison. All around they flapped and glided above the dirty water and every now and then one would swoop down to snatch up some floating piece of edible refuse or give chase to a gull or tern that had picked up a bit of food too large to swallow at once. In its flapping and gliding flight this species is very similar to the Black Kite but it struck me as, perhaps, not quite so buoyant and agile. Its wings appear to beat through a wider arc, giving its flight a rather more laboured appearance.

In Sri Lanka the Brahminy Kite is the only scavenging hawk, but around the harbours and waterways of India, where it is also found, it has to compete with the Black Kite. Although a common scavenger around harbours it is also found about rivers and lakes well away from towns, feeding on frogs, insects, sick fish and other small creatures. It ranges from India east and south to China and northern Australia. The Brahminy Kite's natural habit of taking dead and dying fish, drowning insects and similar flotsam probably predisposed it to sample any scraps of edible offal cast afloat by man. Possibly its habit of chasing other birds which it sees carrying booty also helped it to learn to eat scraps of human food.

New York (1962)

New York is less rich in small parks and green squares than London but it has one very large park – Central Park – which contains not only playing fields, grass, and trees but also quite large areas of scrub woodland, rocky ground, and a sizeable lake. Even although there is plenty of country near New York and there are parks even more extensive and 'wild' only a few kilometres outside the city, Central Park forms a sort of green oasis in a little desert of skyscrapers, and as a result is a wonderful place to see passage migrants. When I first arrived, in early May, the northward migration was in full swing and each morning I saw lots of new and, to me, exciting species on my before-breakfast walk in the park. However, I must here confine myself to the more typical of New York's breeding birds.

Perhaps the most abundant species are the Feral Pigeon and the House Sparrow, both, of course, introduced by man. The former is, as in London and elsewhere, by far the most characteristic bird in the completely built-up areas. In the parks and the gardens around museums and similar places the Starling, also introduced, is much in evidence. All these species fill similar niches to those of their relatives in London.

Everywhere in park and garden, where in London one would expect to see a Blackbird, its new-world counterpart the American Robin is present. Although about the same size and with very similar habits, this thrush is rather shorter-tailed than the British Blackbird and tends to hold itself more upright. It is a handsome bird with dark slate-grey upperparts, streaked throat and chestnut breast. The female is paler and duller than her mate but otherwise similar. In the New York area the Robin is a summer visitor but it comes early and those in Central Park were already breeding when I got there.

To an English ear the short cheerful phrases of the American Robin's song are much inferior to those of our Blackbird (I don't think I am unduly biased in saying this, the song of the American Wood Thrush did enchant me). Its aggressiveness in defence of its nest can be compared with that of the British Mistle Thrush. Not only are Blue Jays and Common Grackles, both about its own size and potential nest robbers, fearlessly attacked if they come anywhere near its nest but the same treatment is given to grey squirrels. Indeed the squirrels were so 'well trained' that they would avoid going anywhere near a Robin's nest even if the bird was not at the moment in evidence! I tried to make a grey squirrel climb a small tree, in which there was a Robin's nest about 3 metres above ground level, by chasing it when it was foraging near the trunk. It started to run up but as soon as it saw the Robin on her nest it turned back and, to my surprise, came down again, clambering over my encircling arms as it did so, and fled over the grass hotly pursued by the male Robin, who had now arrived.

When living under natural conditions the habits of the American

Robin and the type of habitat it chooses are also broadly similar to those of the British Blackbird. It is, however, of all the American thrushes the one that has the widest natural range and which is found in the greatest variety of (woodland) habitats. It was, therefore, in a good position to take advantage of and adapt itself to man-made changes, and had everywhere done so.

The most abundant American bird in Central Park, after the Robin, was the Common Grackle. This is a starling-like bird that belongs to the purely American family Icteridae and is not, in fact, any very close relation to the true starlings of the Old World. The male is somewhat larger than the Starling and has a stouter bill and rather long, graduated tail. The female is smaller and shorter-tailed. She is also slightly duller than the male who is blackish with a rich purple or bronze gloss. In Central Park the Grackles were very conspicuous; strutting over the grass poking and prying for insects in a Starling-like manner, paddling for small fish and aquatic insects at the edge of the lake, coming boldly to visitors for broken peanuts, indulging in their noisy courtship flight, in which several males pursue a female in a chase that is more symbolic display than any deliberate attempt to overtake her, and fussing around their nests in the pine trees.

Of the many American icterids the Common Grackle seems to be pre-eminently the one that is a 'jack of all trades' and so the likeliest to take to town life. That so versatile a bird should adapt to man's presence and learn to live and live well with him is not surprising. But it did surprise me that, in a country so full of starling-like icterids, the European Starling should have been able to establish itself and multiply so greatly. It is often thought that the food supply is the most important factor in controlling the numbers of any bird species but in the case of the introduced Starling in North America there is little evidence of serious competition for food with those native birds which, in part at any rate, take similar foods. The birds which appear to have been adversely affected by the Starling are hole-nesting species such as bluebirds and woodpeckers with which it competes for nesting holes.

In May, Central Park swarms with migrant birds passing through on their way to breeding grounds further north, but of the species that stay and breed there only the Blue Jay seems to qualify as a town bird. I did not find it *much* more numerous than the European Jay is in London but as it is seen often flying about the trees in the streets as well as in parks and as jays are favourite birds of mine, I shall include it here. It is smaller and has a proportionately longer and more graduated tail than the European Jay. It is mainly bluish-mauve above and bright blue, marked with black and white, on wings and tail. I remember once reading, but I forget who wrote it, that if the Blue Jay's breast and underparts were *pure* white it would be the most beautiful bird in the world. I would not go so far as this but certainly it would then be one of the most beautiful. Its underparts are, however, a sort of nebulous and slightly 'dirty-looking' hue that is not quite white nor quite grey nor quite mauve but a bit of each, and to the human eye does seem to detract slightly from its perfection. I hate to be critical of a wild bird's coloration but I must say

I always thought Blue Jays looked best when I was looking down on them, especially if they were in flight with their wonderfully coloured wings and tails spread out.

The Blue Jay is an omnivorous woodland species that can adapt itself to living alongside man provided he leaves plenty of tree cover. Like the European Jay it readily learns to eat artificial foods and it comes even more freely to bird-tables. It is a fairly regular migrant to and from the more northern parts of its range and the majority of the New York birds are, I was told, summer residents only.

CHAPTER THREE

BIRDS FED BY MAN

In one sense it could be argued that man provides food for most of the birds that live with or alongside him, since even 'natural' foods such as the insects and weed seeds in his fields and gardens would not have occurred *in those places*, which would not of course have been fields or gardens, but for man's altering of the environment. I intend, however, to use the above heading in a more restricted sense, that is for birds that feed largely on foods which are provided more directly by man and, but for him, would not be available in anything like their present form or quantity – such foods as plants or animals grown, bred or caught by man for his own use, and foods, like bread, manufactured by him.

Such food, when eaten by birds, usually comes into one of three categories: it may be taken by the birds in spite of man's intention to have it himself; it may be taken only after man has discarded it as waste; or it may be deliberately given to the birds by him. Man's attitude towards the birds he benefits also usually falls into one of three complementary categories. As a rule, he tends to react with resentment and hostility when food he wants is taken, with indifference when food he wastes is eaten, and with pleasure and affection when food he offers is accepted. This generalisation is, however, only broadly true. Most men and women are, like birds, illogical creatures and many factors, quite apart from the 'damage' or lack of it done by a bird, can influence the way people think about it. Man's attitude towards any animal is sometimes independent of the damage it does and depends rather on his preconceived liking or disliking for the creature. People who tolerate Great Tits opening the tops of their milk bottles and sipping the cream might react very differently if Long-tailed Field Mice, let alone Brown Rats, were to do the same thing. Indeed many English people find it very hard to appreciate that some other races of man do not regard small birds as particularly privileged creatures. The very same Englishman may denounce the cruelty of the Tunisians for destroying small birds that ravage their crops, and the 'folly' of the Indians for *not* killing off the scavenging and birds-nesting House Crow!

Food taken

Of the foods that man intends for himself, and of which part are taken by birds before he can get them, the most important consist of cultivated vegetation, particularly grains such as wheat, maize, millet, rice and dari, but also many fruits and some greenstuff. I am here using such terms as 'fruit' and 'seed' in the everyday meaning of these words which is not always the same as the precise botanical meaning.

We can get some idea of the extent to which grain crops benefit certain birds from observation of a field of wheat in England. Let us assume the best sort of situation for the birds, an extensive field that, nevertheless, lies in a 'mixed' landscape with plenty of small woods, copses, odd patches of rough scrub and grassland fairly close to it. Let us assume also that the wheat has not been dressed with poisonous or repellent chemicals and the farmer is too busy or easy-going to do much in the way of bird-scaring.

In March, when the wheat is sown, food is scarce for many birds, especially the seed eaters. Rooks, Jackdaws and Carrion Crows, together with numerous gulls, are attracted when the field is ploughed and search the turned-up earth for exposed insects and worms, and begin to take wheat grains too as soon as the field is sown.

Very soon after the sowing two Stock Doves drop down on the bare earth and walk nimbly and quickly, almost but not quite running, here and there gleaning exposed grains. A Wood Pigeon sees them, circles round, pitches on a tall elm at the edge of the field, and after sitting for some time in nervous hesitation joins them. Other Wood Pigeons that pass over see it feeding and they too come down; and a pair of Feral Pigeons from the town a couple of kilometres away joins them. Next day all these birds, remembering where they fed so well, fly back to the field in a decisive and confident manner that induces many others, who were less successful on the previous day, to follow them. By that afternoon there are almost as many pigeons on the field as there are crows. The pigeons, however, take only exposed grains, many of which would fail to germinate successfully in any case, only now and then scratching aside some of the soil with their bills where it is very loose and fairly dry. The Crows and Jackdaws and even more the Rooks, on the other hand, do a fair amount of digging and turn over quite large clods of earth.

Chaffinches and Yellow Buntings search in scattered parties, hopping over the clods and fleeing to the surrounding hedges or wood-edge or the large elm tree at each sign of danger. House Sparrows, although much more numerous, tend to keep more to the edge of the field and flee back to the shelter of the hedge in a minor panic every few minutes. Locally Corn Buntings and Tree Sparrows may also join in searching for the new-sown wheat. Starling flocks also come and may take a considerable amount of grain if they are not successful at finding insect food. In some of the Shetland Islands in Scotland the Starling is looked upon as one of the worst scourges of the new-sown grainfields, although in other places the more obvious grain-eating of Rooks, Wood Pigeons and House Sparrows most rouses the farmer's anger. A few 'old-fashioned' farmers may resignedly quote the old grain-sowing rhyme 'One for the pigeon, one for the crow, two to rot and one to grow', but the attitude therein implied is growing rarer in our modern civilisations.

As soon as the wheat, or what is left of it, has fairly begun to grow it is, for a period, usually safe from attack by birds. It is true that many species may peck and eat the growing tip of young wheat, but most do this only to a small extent and prefer the shoots of grasses or buds of trees which are then also to be had in quantity. In a few places wild geese or the introduced Canada Goose may graze on the growing wheat, as may Mute Swans if the field borders some river or lake where they are numerous. Mostly, however, birds do not molest the growing wheat nor, consequently, do they benefit from it, except in so far as it may provide cover for ground-dwelling species such as the Quail and the Pheasant.

As soon, however, as the grains in the ear begin to 'fill out' and while they are still soft and milky inside the grain-eating birds start to feed on them. Large flocks of House Sparrows gather in the hedge, fly into the corn and, clinging to the stems, remove the grains from ear after ear. Greenfinches and Tree Sparrows may join in the feast but their numbers are usually small compared with those of the House Sparrows. Wood Pigeons also take the ripening grains from the ears, clinging awkwardly to the stems, often spreading out their wings against the vegetation for support, just as they do when hanging in the peripheral twigs of a tree to pluck berries or acorns. If, as often happens, patches of the crop are 'laid' or flattened by rainstorms, playing dogs, badgers, or courting humans, this gives the Wood Pigeons a more comfortable place to feed. It also encourages species which do not usually settle in standing corn such as Rooks, Carrion Crows, Jackdaws, Stock Doves and Feral Pigeons, to alight and feed. When a wheatfield has been largely 'laid' by thunderstorms it is often black with Rooks shortly afterwards and much of the grain is lost to them.

A recently-cut wheatfield supplies, as a rule, a main food for all the local Rooks, Wood Pigeons, Feral Pigeons, Stock Doves, House Sparrows and Jackdaws, and a usually much smaller proportion of their diet for some other birds such as Carrion Crows and Magpies as well. Where such a field is left to lie fallow the birds still find wheat on it far into the winter, while the weeds that grew up in the cover of the corn and ripened after it was cut, and others that grew after the field was reaped, also supply a great deal of seed food. Throughout many parts of the world as far apart as Ireland and Tibet, the stubble fields supply a stand-by for many birds during the autumn and winter months. Nowadays, however, at any rate in 'advanced' countries, it is increasingly the custom to use combine harvesters. These seem to spill even more grain than the old methods but they have two great disadvantages so far as many birds are concerned. First, they leave the cut corn with a longer stalk and so render the stubble field a less convenient foraging ground for such birds as Rooks and Stock Doves that like to feed unimpeded by vegetation. More serious, however, is the fact that the straw so left is considered worthless and so it is the practice to burn it and with it, of course, the wheat, the weed seeds and the insects as well. Where this is done the seed-eating birds can often get little more wheat from that field, although the grains that have been only 'toasted' are readily eaten.

Throughout the world seed-eating birds, of some kind or another, batten on man's grain crops. In the small, roughly cleared millet fields of Zaire parties of the lovely little Black-capped Waxbills cling to the growing sprays, picking out the seeds. In other parts of Africa where modern methods produce large areas of rice or dari vast flocks of Red-billed Weavers or Queleas come to feed on the grain. In the high Tibetan valleys Choughs, Snow Pigeons and Eastern Rock Pigeons glean the stony, wind-swept fields all through the bitter winter for grain and weed seeds. If modern methods were to spread to Tibet (as they may have done now under Communist China's rule) and the fields were fired after harvest, it would almost certainly bring about a decrease in the numbers of these three species. In eastern North America, in spring, every little wayside pool, far more every fairly extensive swamp, is enlivened and beautified by the Red-winged Blackbird, an icterid to whose spectacular 'fire and night' brilliance the average American bird-watcher is as indifferent as is his English counterpart to the beauty of the Wood Pigeon. After the breeding season Red-winged Blackbirds flock to the grainfields and it is thought that their present great abundance is due to the extensive monoculture of cereals.

In Britain the amount of fruit taken by birds tends to be over-looked, by most of us, anyway, even if not always by *professional* fruit growers. One reason for this is, I think, that the birds which do most damage to fruit in Britain, such as the Starling, Blackbird and to a lesser extent the Song Thrush, Mistle Thrush and Blackcap, are song birds (in both the popular and the ornithological senses of the word). Public opinion in England thinks it admirable to kill game-birds and waterfowl for sport but cruel to kill song birds, even for food, as the Mediterranean and African peasants do. Personally I am quite out of sympathy with this attitude, but that may be because I get as great a thrill from the beauty of a Pheasant or a Man-darin Drake as I do from the song of a Skylark or a Blackbird. In Europe, in any case, the taking of fruit by birds does not usually have any serious repercussions on man. In some areas, however, things are otherwise. For example in parts of Tunisia the olive harvest, which is the main support of the people, may be ruined by the vast wintering flocks of Starlings from northern and eastern Europe.

Buds and flowers are eaten by many birds, and the latter may be incidentally destroyed by honey-eating birds, such as the brush-tongued parrots called lories and lorikeets, in their search for nectar and pollen. The British Bullfinch is notoriously a bud eater and in some years fruit buds are locally an important part of its food in late winter and early spring.

In Britain the larger birds-of-prey, and indeed most of the smaller species also, have long been greatly reduced in numbers. The same is true in most other countries where people are 'thick on the ground' and well-off enough to own shot-guns. This and the fact that our poultry are now mostly mass-produced in buildings and not, as at one time, kept in small numbers around farms and in villages, makes it easy for us to overlook or even deny the appreciable damage done to domestic poultry by birds-of-prey, both in Britain in former days and in less 'advanced' parts of the world today.

A glance at olden literature, however, shows how omnipresent and resented were the depredations of the Kite, now existing in Britain only as a pitiful and protected remnant in central Wales but then a common scavenger and poultry 'thief'. In Shakespeare's *Macbeth*, when Macduff learns that his wife and children have been murdered he cries 'What? hell kite all? What? all my pretty chickens and their dam at one fell swoop?' Another writer describes in a poem how the good wives of the village complain bitterly 'of chicken, duck and gosling gone astray; all fallen a prey to the sweeping kite'. Elsewhere in Europe the Black Kite and the Goshawk were also often serious predators on domestic poultry. Probably, in most cases, the damage done to the economy as a whole was not, to use modern jargon, 'of economic significance' but even so it was a serious matter for some poor hen-wife when a Kite or Goshawk came day after day to her yard for a chicken.

Food discarded

Besides the food that he intends to use but does not always manage to keep entirely for himself, man discards considerable quantities of food in such manner that it becomes available for birds – also of course, in many cases, for other animals which will not be mentioned here except in so far as they may affect the availability of such foods to birds. I include as discarded both food deliberately discarded by man, such as crusts of bread thrown into the gutter, or sick or senile domestic animals driven out to die, and food which is accidentally discarded, such as the grain spilled when it is being loaded into trucks or storage depots or the unsaleable fish that have been caught willy-nilly in a trawl along with commercially valued species and are thrown back into the sea.

Food discarded by man is not, as is often thought, available only in countries where most people are reasonably well fed and can afford to buy as much as they want, at any rate of the cheaper sorts of foods. In many of the poorer parts of the world the towns not only, like ours, support populations of birds that largely live by scavenging, but large numbers of feral dogs as well. Usually the main reason for this is that, owing to lack of modern methods of garbage disposal, more of the edible or partly edible scraps are thrown into the streets or on to waste ground in the immediate vicinity. Sometimes the dietary customs of the people prevent certain things being used for human food; for example, pious Hindus do not eat beef and so in India dead cattle are commonly left for the dogs and vultures after the leather workers have removed the hide.

The carcasses of domestic animals are the largest items of food that are sometimes discarded by man on land and serve to feed the largest and most spectacular of the birds that benefit from his leavings – the vultures. Modern civilisation is, however, hard on vultures; not only are they quite unreasonably disliked and despised (for why should we dislike or despise a bird because its way of life, unlike our own, does not involve killing other creatures?) but modern ideas about efficiency and hygiene result in few, if any, carcasses being left lying about. This at least is the case in the more densely-populated parts of technically 'advanced' countries.

On the other hand more primitive methods of animal husbandry very often result in there being more food for vultures than before man came on the scene. Weak and sickly animals may die far from their owners' houses or tents and are not recovered. Exhausted beasts of burden are left to die and become food for any animal that finds them. This happens of course only when the owners, as is often the case, either have plenty of better animals for their own food and so do not bother about a worn-out old ox or donkey or when their religion forbids them to use its flesh. The provision of such carcasses is not always the only benefit that man brings. Very often, to safeguard his flocks and herds, he has killed off or reduced the numbers of predatory and scavenging large mammals which would otherwise often prevent vultures from feeding on a carcass. An ornithologist who travelled in north-eastern Tibet in the 1930s gave a graphic account of how he watched a single wolf that for a whole day alternately fed from and guarded the carcass of a sheep, successfully keeping off scores of Himalayan Griffon Vultures that were gathered around hoping for a chance to feed.

The larger vultures are, generally speaking, specialised carcass feeders and it is only where man discards animal or human bodies that they can successfully batten on his handiwork. The same is, however, not true for some of the smaller species such as the Hooded Vulture and the Egyptian Vulture. At a carcass these cannot compete with the scrum of larger vultures, so they scavenge around picking up small pieces and scraps that the others let fall. They also take any more or less helpless small creatures that come in their way. Given this type of feeding behaviour it is easy to see how some of them, although no doubt originally attracted to man's vicinity by carcasses and the attendant larger vultures, have become scavengers around human habitations. Here they have learnt to eat almost any scraps of edible refuse of animal origin, and in some places where there are now few carcasses to be had these smaller vultures still eke out a living in the gutters and on the garbage heaps.

One of the two widespread and locally common small vultures of the Americas, the Black Vulture, has in this way managed to become quite a successful scavenger. The other, the Turkey Vulture, has in modern times found a new source of food in the bodies of the many small creatures killed on the roads. On the whole this seems to be to its advantage, although when getting this food some

Black Vultures on a rubbish dump in Trinidad. This small vulture is as characteristic a scavenger on refuse tips in many parts of tropical America as is the far
more beautiful Herring Gull in Britain. (*Cyril Walker*)

individuals suffer the same fate as that of their prospective dinner.
Incidentally these and the other American vultures, which include
the spectacular Condor and the beautiful King Vulture, are now
thought, rightly in my opinion, not to be related to the old world
vultures, which are close relatives of the hawks and eagles, but to
have come to look like them through having evolved to fill the same
role of carrion feeders in their respective homelands.

Kites are often spoken of, or at any rate written about in stories
with an eastern setting, as if they were primarily feeders on large
carcasses, human and otherwise. In Rudyard Kipling's *Jungle Books*
Chil the kite was always 'waiting for things to die'. In fact, although
they may at times feed from corpses their role is rather that of
snatchers up of any morsel of flesh or offal that the larger carrion

feeders let fall. They have, as I described in the chapter on birds in towns, become hangers-on about towns and villages in many parts of the old world. The Kite or Red Kite once scavenged in English towns, the (so-called) Black Kite still does so in many eastern towns and the beautiful Brahminy Kite, that so delighted me during my brief visit to Sri Lanka, scavenges the shores and waterways from India to New Guinea.

Crows, like kites, are pickers up of trifles rather than carrion feeders. Many of them are, however, very ready to feed from the carcasses of dead large animals if they get the chance. Usually they do not do so unless some other creature such as a fox, wolf or vulture has torn it open. It is, however, probable that the Raven, which is the largest and most spectacular of all the crows, if we except two African species – the White-necked Raven and the Thick-billed Raven – has always been in part a carcass feeder. It has long taken advantage of man's provision of carcasses, human or otherwise. Its tendency to put in an appearance on battlefields, its sepulchral croaking and uniform glossy black plumage, its intelligence and its strong but elegant flight have combined to impress mankind and there is, as a result, a wealth of myth and folklore about it. It was held sacred to the Norse god Odin who had two Ravens, Thought and Memory, which flew about the world all day and came back at night to roost on their master's shoulders and tell him everything that had happened. In the Noah's ark story and in an even earlier flood legend – the epic of Gilgamesh – a Raven plays a prominent if not (from the human viewpoint) entirely admirable part and it is probable that it was one of the birds that was used, no doubt often with success, as a land-finding bird by seafarers in very early days.

Land-finding birds were, apparently, kept captive on board, released if and when the ship had gone off its course and none knew the direction of the nearest land, and then followed. Probably the Raven's use in this sphere was due to its being easily kept alive and healthy enough to fly strongly when released. This bird will live and even thrive, at least for some time, on a régime that would soon reduce a Rook or Carrion Crow to the sort of pathetic travesty of its wild relatives that we too often see in zoos.

The Australian Raven is much more closely related to the other Australian crows than it is to the northern Raven to which, however, it shows considerable convergent resemblance. It also has elongated throat feathers which it erects to form a sort of beard or feathery dewlap when in self-assertive mood, it is also partly a carrion feeder when it gets the chance, ever ready to come to the carcasses of large mammals and, like the northern Raven, not always averse to helping to bring death to foundered sheep or sickly lambs. It is also a superlative if not quite so spectacular flyer but its voice, particularly a characteristic long-drawn-out series of 'dying-away' calls uttered in a most despairing tone, tends to be lugubrious rather than sepulchral. The Australian Raven, like its very close relatives the Australian Crow, the Little Crow and the Little Raven, probably long ago learned to scavenge at Aboriginal camp-sites and still does so in many places. All these species have, in most places, now learned that modern man with his gun is a good deal more dangerous than primitive man. They have, however, adapted well to the opening up of Australia and are common scavengers in and around most outback towns.

In Britain the popular dislike of crows prevents their battening as closely on man as they might otherwise do. However, the Carrion Crow, Rook, Jackdaw and, where they occur, the Hooded Crow and Raven, feed in numbers on garbage tips. In some places Rooks and Jackdaws scavenge for scraps around large railway stations (although not usually coming right into the stations as do House Sparrows and pigeons) and at places where people habitually picnic.

In May 1976, I stayed on the south coast of England in Weymouth, at an hotel that overlooked the promenade. Here the local Rooks were much bolder than I have known them elsewhere. They thoroughly ransacked the litter baskets on the promenade in the early morning. One Monday morning I saw, to my surprise, Rooks obtain, from one basket, one entire half and two wing-pieces of cooked chicken (apparently quite uneaten by their human purchasers), one chicken leg with only a little meat left, an unopened cellophane packet of sandwiches (which took the Rook that got it some time and effort to break open), a half-full bag of crisps, two papers containing a few fried potatoes and several part-eaten sandwiches. Both the Carrion and Hooded Crows also, in places, habitually visit camps and picnic sites as soon as the people move away, to scavenge any edible scraps they have left. In those parts of the world where they are not particularly disliked by man many crows, of differing species, commonly scavenge about towns and villages and one of them, the House Crow of India and Sri Lanka, is a regular hanger-on of mankind.

The modern tendency, at least in countries such as our own, is for waste to be carted away and dumped on official garbage tips. These are usually in fairly open country and at a little distance from the nearest human habitation. In Britain most garbage tips are regularly visited not only by the crows but also by large numbers of Starlings, House Sparrows and gulls. All British breeding gulls – Greater Black-backed, Lesser Black-backed, Herring, Common and Black-headed – are to be seen in such places. Indeed, even gulls that are rather rare visitors, such as the Glaucous Gull, or occasional vagrants such as the beautiful Ivory Gull, may turn up in such places.

It is a fine spectacle to see the gulls descend to feed on some large tip, rising up with a flashing of hundreds of grey and white, black and white and mottled brown wings when one of the garbage trucks comes too near and then descending in a screaming, snatching, threatening, rummaging, grabbing, tugging, gulping throng when it has dumped its load. Unfortunately the officials in charge usually forbid entry to municipal garbage dumps and try to locate the dumping area or to screen it with fences so that the bird-watcher cannot overlook it. Often, however, they are unable to do this and one can get good views of the gulls and other birds on the dump from some roadway or public land nearby, provided one has a good pair of binoculars. The amount of edible waste thrown out on garbage tips has probably been a significant factor in the general increase of gulls in Europe and America, and in increasing the number of gulls wintering inland in Britain.

Although gulls nowadays take their share of food discarded on land we think of them as typically gleaners of food discarded at sea or on its shore. Wherever and whenever fishing is or has been practised gulls, of whatever species are locally found, have usually learnt to come and feed on the wastage, whether this consists of the vast amounts of unsaleable species of fish hosed back dead or dying into the sea from the deck of some trawler or the few dozen heads and guts discarded after he brings his catch to shore by some more primitively-equipped individual fisherman. The majority of gulls are naturally gleaners of dead and dying fish and other creatures along the tidelines (although most of them catch some surface-swimming fish by dipping or plunge diving also, and some are partly insectivorous), and so this role of scavenger has not necessitated any great change in behaviour on their part. Indeed, long before there were ships, gulls were probably in the habit, as they still are today, of following seals, porpoises and other large sea mammals in order to snatch bits of their prey when they fed or to seize fish driven to the surface by them. Gulls also follow liners and other non–fishing vessels in order to pick up the scraps thrown out from the galleys. Some people imagine that the same gulls have followed their ship day after day but this they seldom, probably never, do. Watching from shipboard one finds that any gull one can recognise as an individual seldom keeps behind for very long. If no food has been thrown out for some time the following gulls are very apt to fly off to any other ship that comes in sight, often passing en route and being replaced by others that have, evidently, been following *that* ship without reward! Terns, being more specialised and skilful catchers of fish than gulls and less catholic in tastes, have not benefited so much from the fish-catching and food–discarding of man. Two species at least have, however, done so locally. In Iceland, in summer, Arctic Terns habitually scavenge for fish scraps and in Colombo Harbour the Whiskered Tern picks up small floating scraps of edible refuse as well as small dead fish.

Gulls are not the only sea-birds that take advantage of man's wastefulness, and really far from land they are not the most numerous of those that do so. Here some of the more truly pelagic tube-noses or Procellariiformes, the petrels, shearwaters and albatrosses, largely take over the role of scavengers around fishing boats. One petrel that does so in the northern oceans is the Fulmar. This bird now breeds round the coast of most of Britain, nesting on ledges and sometimes even on top of ruined crofts or in niches about buildings near the sea. Although its grey and white plumage gives it a superficially gull-like appearance, its bulky head and body with large dark eye and distinctive flight with long, sweeping glides punctuated by a few stiff-winged wing beats, at once identify it.

The Fulmar feeds on various small marine creatures that it picks up on or near the surface, and on any floating fatty offal or carrion that it can find. In the early days of whaling, when the formerly plentiful whales of the Arctic were first being exploited by man, Fulmars gathered in hundreds round the whaling ships feasting on the lumps of fat and flesh drifting about and even tearing at the skinned carcasses. Later, when the whales were so reduced in number that the northern whaling industry petered out, the Fulmar was able to turn to the waste of the fishing trawlers which had by then begun to venture further north and further from shore. James Fisher, whose book on the Fulmar can be heartily recommended to anyone interested in sea-birds, was convinced as a result of his investigations that the great increase of the Fulmar's numbers and its spread southward during the last century has been due chiefly to its making use of this source of *extra* food which first the whalers and then the fishermen provided for it. The present greater need for human foods and fertilisers owing to the continual increase of mankind is, however, leading to a tendency for trawlers to make use of *all* their catch in some way or other. If such practice becomes universal it is likely that the Fulmar will decline.

In the southern oceans a persistent scavenger of the whaling industry is or perhaps, in view of the present state of the whaling industry, one must say 'was' the black and white, spotted-winged Cape Pigeon – a petrel about the size of the British Fulmar although very unlike it in appearance. Vast numbers of Cape Pigeons may be attracted by the easy pickings of a whaling station and the closing down of such a place, either temporarily for the duration of the Antarctic winter or permanently as a result of the recent tendency of some nations to give up their whaling industries, often results in the death by starvation of large numbers of Cape Pigeons which have been suddenly cast on their own resources. It is probable that in this and other oceanic species, it is normal for many immature birds to die of starvation during prolonged bad weather or at times of year when natural foods are in short supply. When man supplies additional food many young that would otherwise have died survive. It is, therefore, likely that the large-scale mortality of Cape Pigeons following the closure of a whaling station does not, pitiful though it is, represent an 'extra' man-made loss to the species' numbers but only the death of a number that would have died earlier in their lives *but* for man's activities.

Some albatrosses, including the gigantic Wandering Albatross which may have a wingspan of nearly 4 metres, and some of the smaller species, such as the Black-browed Albatross, which are commonly called 'mollymawks' or 'mollies' by sailors, habitually follow ships; at least they did so in the days of sail and the early days of steam, but modern ships tend to go too fast for them. Albatrosses, although superb gliders in windy weather, are much less agile than gulls or the smaller petrels and usually alight on the water to feed, taking only larger pieces of floating fishy or fatty refuse. It is unlikely that ships have ever been a very important source of food to any albatross as a species, although they may have been to a few individuals. I regret to say that the supposed superstitious sanctity of the albatross seems to have originated with Coleridge's famous poem; the old-time sailors caught them on fishing lines baited with lumps of salt pork trailed behind the boat and killed them without compunction or fear of any ill luck in consequence!

Two further sources of discarded food are seeds that are spilled accidentally and bits of waste food dropped or thrown away by people. Wherever grain is stored and moved into or out of storage some of it is usually spilled. This is particularly the case in countries where grain is still shifted largely by hand, and when grain is ground in the open by more or less primitive means as in, for example, some African and Asian villages.

Some small seed-eating passerine birds and a few species of pigeons benefit from seed spilled in this way. In Africa three birds that do so are the Common or Senegal Firefinch, the House Bunting and the Laughing Dove. The Firefinch is a tiny bird, smaller than the British Wren. The male is mainly scarlet to brownish mauve-red in colour (there is much geographical variation – firefinches from arid tropical regions are brighter than those from further south) and the female brown with a red rump and a red stripe over her eye. The Common Firefinch has a wide distribution in tropical and sub-tropical Africa. It is naturally a bird of fairly dry bushy places where there are tangles of thorny cover, but in most of its range it has become adapted to living in villages with man. Here it hops around, often feeding partly on spilled grains of millet or fragments of rice that it picks out of the dust but also taking seeds of wild grasses and small insects. The 'natural' site for its nest is in a bush or shrub but it is nowadays often placed in some nook in or on a building and lined with the feathers of the Domestic Fowl.

The House Bunting is an unpretentious-looking streaky brown bird, very like the British Reed Bunting in general appearance, but with a striped head. It is found in arid and rocky semi-desert regions in northern Africa and eastwards through parts of the Middle East to Pakistan and India. Throughout the Saharan parts of its range it also lives alongside man in villages and towns. It forages for scattered seeds and crumbs around the houses and comes freely inside them if it gets the chance. One trait that has helped it to live successfully with man (or perhaps developed in adaptation as a consequence of living with him) is that it is quick to take alarm but does not remain frightened for long. One ornithologist has compared its behaviour to that of the house fly in this respect because he observed it return again and again no matter how many times it was frightened away. It is obvious, however, that a bird which behaves like this can only succeed where the people are either very tolerant of it or very inefficient in their attempts to get rid of it. Perhaps this is one reason why the House Bunting has not followed man widely about the world as has the House Sparrow, on whom hostile actions from man make a more lasting impression.

The Laughing Dove which was mentioned in an earlier chapter (p. 74) is a common village bird throughout Africa and usually feeds partly on grain (largely various millets) spilled by man. Other seed-eating passerines and pigeons behave rather similarly in different parts of the world. Where breads and similar 'artificial' foods form a large part of the human diet and crumbs are let fall, as they usually are, such birds often learn to take these man-made foods as well as grain. As we see in the case of the British House Sparrow and Feral Pigeon this stands them in good stead when, as often happens in the course of 'modernisation', towns increase in size but the transport and marketing of grain becomes either restricted to limited areas or ceases altogether.

Foods given

We now come to the third category: birds which benefit from food that man deliberately gives to them. This he may do for many different reasons. He may believe the birds he feeds are holy and that by feeding them he gains the goodwill of supernatural powers; he may do it as a convenient way of disposing of waste food (although this is probably very rarely the *only* reason for feeding birds); he may wish to attract birds to a certain place in order to study them, or he may be fond of birds for sentimental or aesthetic reasons and wish to try to help them. Often more than one reason works in combination or there may be transition from one reason to another in the course of time. In former days many people in Britain considered the Robin as one of God's particular bird favourites (the Wren being another) and thus had religious motives for succouring it, but it is likely that these religious beliefs grew up around the Robin *after* and not before its beauty and confiding ways had endeared it to at least one imaginative person. Incidentally, these ideas about the Robin's special status were quite widespread as late as the 1930s. I vividly recall a schoolmate of mine, who habitually shot and trapped all other possible birds, from Chaffinches to Turtledoves, to feed his ferrets, coming to school one morning genuinely distressed and worried because he had shot a Robin by accident!

The ancient Greeks were horrified at the thought of their bodies or those of their friends being eaten by dogs or birds, although ready enough to consign the bodies of their enemies to this use. So far as I know there are no peoples, past or present, who have ever willingly fed dogs or other mammals with their corpses. The idea of being eaten by birds does not usually seem to repel people to the same extent, however, probably because birds are often regarded as symbols of the soul or of immortality. At least two highly-cultured peoples feed birds deliberately with the bodies of their dead, or certainly until very recently did so.

The Parsees of India erect tall towers, called, so I am told, 'towers of silence'. The body is put on a grille at the top of the tower. Here vultures, perhaps with occasional help from Black Kites, feed on the flesh and the remaining bones are later buried. In parts of Tibet human corpses are, or at least were up till the time of the Chinese occupation, disposed of by breaking them up and feeding them to the vultures (the Himalayan Griffon being the species chiefly benefiting). In both cases the idea behind the custom seems to have been that man should make a last gift of his body to some other living creatures. To me it seems at least as reasonable to feed birds soon after one's death as to feed bacteria after a rather longer period and much pleasanter than the ancient Egyptian and modern Russian ideas of trying to preserve some human corpses indefinitely.

If the custom of feeding of Robins in winter started in Britain only after the bird had gained a mythical religious significance, then it is likely that the present-day widespread feeding of birds in this country was religious in origin, as the Robin seems to have been the first wild species to have been *given* food as distinct from being enticed into traps or snares by means of bait. Certainly the Scandinavian custom of putting out a sheaf of corn for the birds at Christmas was, almost undoubtedly, a religious as well as a benevolent act.

Long before anyone thought of feeding them, birds would have tended to gather round human dwellings in hard weather. Grain-eating species would have been attracted by the grains spilled or fed to domestic animals or poultry. Also all birds that feed on the ground are attracted by snow-free areas when all else is snow-covered, and the activities of men, pigs and poultry would have ensured that there were always such areas about houses. In hard winters in England a 'mistaken' example of this instinct can sometimes be seen when flocks of starving Skylarks drop down on to the snow-less but also food-less streets of our modern cities. Thus, in hard winters, there would always have been hungry wild birds about, ready to touch the heart of any susceptible person. At one time the use most commonly made of the plight of birds in hard weather was to catch them to eat or, less often, to cage them. It is only in the last seventy years or so that, even in Britain and North America, the idea that it is wrong to kill passerine birds for food, although right to kill waterfowl and game-birds for pleasure, has become widespread. The use of birds for food and as pets from earliest times was, however, an important factor in enabling them, or some of them, to reach their present privileged position with us. Creatures that we keep as pets, or even those we eat, are not, however harmful or troublesome they may sometimes be, looked upon as despicable and unclean.

The habit of feeding wild birds is now widespread in northern and central Europe and in North America, as well as in Britain. People take food into large parks in towns, town squares or, at least in London, to the river's edge and feed the birds; when they are eating at open-air restaurants, street coffee stalls or similar places they throw pieces of food to birds that have learnt to gather round; last and most important of all, perhaps, they put out food for birds in their gardens.

In Britain feeding in town parks is probably of most importance to waterfowl (chiefly the Mallard and, in winter, the Tufted Duck), gulls, Feral Pigeons, Wood Pigeons, Blackbirds, Starlings and House Sparrows. The numbers of all these would be much reduced (in most town parks) if people brought no food for them. Other small birds in some parks also rely partly on food given to them by the public. In Kew Gardens and Holland Park, for example, Coal Tits, Great Tits, Blue Tits, Robins, Chaffinches and Nuthatches will all come for peanuts or bits of cheese (and in hard times for bread also) and some of them will take food from the hand. In many parks in Europe, such as those in and around Vienna and Oslo, it is customary for people to feed birds and Red Squirreis, and also to put 'official' supplies of sunflower and other seeds in snow-proof open-fronted boxes fixed to stumps or trees. I think it very likely that this results in a larger population of tits and Nuthatches, to say nothing of House and Tree Sparrows, than would otherwise be possible. I have certainly nowhere seen Great Tits and Nuthatches so abundant and so tame as in the grounds of the Schönbrunn Palace near Vienna.

Open-air restaurants are often much patronised by the local birds as well as by their clients. On Box Hill, in Surrey, there was, and may still be, a café with outside tables where the local tits and Chaffinches come for food. In London the many open-air coffee stalls and similar establishments make a significant contribution to the food supply of Feral Pigeons and House Sparrows. Among the clientèle of any London coffee stall there are usually a number of customers, some of them by no means well-off or well-fed themselves, who share their meals with the birds.

Feeding birds in one's garden, or on one's windowsill if one is so unfortunate as not to have even the smallest of backyards, is very popular in Britain. It is equally so in many parts of Europe and in North America. In Britain the species that benefit most from this garden feeding are the Blackbird, Robin, Great Tit, Blue Tit, Starling, Greenfinch, House Sparrow and Collared Dove. There can, I think, be no doubt that the numbers of all these species, especially the Blackbird, Starling and House Sparrow, would decrease considerably if all feeding of birds by individual garden owners were suddenly to cease. In addition to the above species the Song Thrush, Dunnock, Coal Tit, Nuthatch, Chaffinch and Greater Spotted Woodpecker all commonly take food put out for them. Probably they also are, as a result, more plentiful than they would otherwise be but not, I think, to the same extent as the species in the first list.

On the continent of Europe the garden-fed birds are mostly the same species although the Nuthatch and Coal Tit often take more prominent roles, the Tree Sparrow is a much more habitual guest at 'bird-tables' than in Britain and, locally, the Marsh Tit and even the rather rare and extremely beautiful Middle Spotted Woodpecker may regularly come for handouts.

In North America tits are also prominent among the bird-table birds, especially the Black-capped Chickadee, a species very like a greyer edition of the British Willow Tit and at one time thought to be the same species. Nuthatches are also common garden visitors in the U.S.A., as is the little Downy Woodpecker, unlike its English counterpart the Lesser Spotted Woodpecker. So also are several finches, the drab Pine Siskin, the Purple Finch, the Hawfinch-like Evening Grosbeak and the crimson, crested Cardinal. This last species, which may be more closely related to the buntings than to the true finches, has now extended its range northwards and occurs in larger numbers than formerly in the more northerly parts of its range. This is generally, and I believe correctly, ascribed to its now feeding largely at bird-tables in winter.

Although it is hardly a garden bird it seems a good place, while talking of birds that are fed by man in Europe, to mention the Alpine Chough. About Jackdaw-size, black with dull red legs and a rather slender yellow bill, this high-mountain bird is an even more superlative flyer than the Raven. In summer it stays mostly at very high altitudes and supplements its natural diet of insects, molluscs, and berries with handouts from picnickers. In winter it feeds at lower levels around human dwellings, foraging on garbage heaps and coming to windows for food offered to it. What it did before the Alps became so densely populated, or what it does in winter now in those parts of its range, such as the Himalayas and south-eastern Europe, where people are fewer and less affluent, does not seem to have been recorded.

When birds depend on food deliberately given to them by man their food supply is likely to be even more capricious than that of birds dependent on man's leavings. The coffee stall that supplies the local House Sparrows and Feral Pigeons, and the buildings where they nest, may be bulldozed away to clear space to erect a modern civic centre or a block of battery flats; the old lady who has fed the birds in her garden regularly and generously for the past forty years dies and those who take over her home have 'no time for all that sentimental nonsense'. One can see many examples such as these and, of course, many to the contrary.

In one respect, however, birds that rely on food *given* to them may, and very often do, have a unique advantage. Birds dependent on natural foods or on foods taken or discarded by man are forced to adjust their numbers to their food supply or, to put it more correctly, their numbers are forcibly adjusted to the food supply by natural processes. When people are *giving* food to birds, however, they usually do not like to see any of their suppliants go away hungry. If twice as many tits and Nuthatches come to a bird-table now as came a month ago it is likely that twice as much food will be put on it for them. Many more people will come and give food to a hundred pigeons waiting about in a town square than will do so where there are only four or five pigeons. So that, unlike any other bird populations, birds relying on human charity *may* be lucky enough to have their food supply increase and keep pace with their increasing numbers. The nearest approach to this in the wild state, so far as I know, is the spreading and perpetuating of the plants or trees which feed them by birds such as thrushes, tanagers and fruit pigeons that swallow fruits and berries and then disgorge or pass their seeds

unharmed, and by nutcrackers and many species of jays and tits, which hide seeds in the ground and do not recover all of them. Very often, of course, when people are giving food, there is an upper limit to the amount of food that can, with the best will in the world, be supplied. If more and more Starlings and House Sparrows come to the garden the bird feeder is usually forced, sooner or later, to stop increasing his or her bounty. Birds fed by man may also find their food supply dwindle almost to nothing should war, or some other calamity that causes widespread shortage of food, strike the people on whose charity they rely.

CHAPTER FOUR

INTRODUCED BIRDS

When, in May 1941, the troopship in which I was on passage to the Middle East put in to Durban Harbour, I looked eagerly at some little birds hopping about on the wharf. To my disappointment they were no exotic species, only the familiar House Sparrow. A little smaller and more brightly coloured than English specimens, they were in fact the Indian race of the species. They owed their presence in South Africa to introduction by man, as did another Indian bird, the Common or House Myna which I found to be one of the most conspicuous species when I got ashore.

When they colonised distant continents many homesick immigrants were eager to have about them the familiar birds of their native lands. Some ornithologists were also interested in the possibility of introducing species to new countries. As a result not only did many private individuals attempt to introduce birds to lands where they did not naturally occur, but many 'acclimatisation societies' were set up, often under the highest auspices, for the purpose of so doing. It is always easy to be wise after the event, but at least more people might have anticipated that those species most likely to succeed at living with man in the new countries were those that had most successfully done so in the old, and reflected that these were by no means universally approved of even at home. Now the pendulum of opinion, or at least the opinion of most officials and ornithologists, has swung far the other way and authorities are usually hostile to the suggestion of introducing *any* foreign bird or mammal. In some countries, however, they make exceptions where 'sporting birds' are involved and permit or even encourage the introduction of such species as the Pheasant and the Chukar Partridge.

To give some idea of the effects of introductions, I intend to list some different parts of the world and discuss briefly their introduced birds, or at least some of them.

North America

Here the Starling and the House Sparrow are the outstanding successes. Both fill essentially the same role as they do in Europe and both, once they got going, successfully overcame attempts to reduce their numbers or halt their advance. Early attempts to introduce the Starling failed but after sixty were freed in Central Park in 1890 and forty more in 1891, the species throve beyond its sponsors' wildest hopes. Of the many other passerine birds deliberately or accidentally introduced only a few have had any success and that of a more limited nature. The Tree Sparrow established itself around St Louis where twelve pairs were liberated in 1870. It has, however, done little more than hold its own, probably as a result of competition from the House Sparrow.

The House Finch a native of Mexico and the hot, dry parts of the south-western U.S.A., was introduced into Long Island (no one seems quite sure when or by whom) and maintains a rather pre-carious population there and it is also said to occur, in places, from Connecticut to Maryland. It looks rather like a large and thick-billed Redpoll, streaky brown with a red forehead and breast, and is very much a town and village bird in its native haunts. The Goldfinch was an early candidate for American citizenship. Innumerable attempts to introduce it seemed at last to have succeeded and it became locally common in and around New York. Then it apparently vanished, only to appear again many years later in Long Island, where it now appears, however, to be extinct.

The Skylark has even more romantic and literary associations than the Goldfinch, although it never had the latter's religious signifi-cance. Naturally, therefore, determined efforts were also made to establish it on American soil. As with the Goldfinch, most of these attempts proved unsuccessful. Small local populations maintained themselves for twenty to thirty years on Long Island and near Port-land in Oregon but now the Skylark's only outpost in America is on the southern tip of Vancouver Island in British Columbia. Here it inhabits farmland essentially similar to that which it has long colonised throughout its European range.

The Crested Myna, a species of far-eastern starling, has become established around Vancouver in British Columbia but has not, as yet, managed to extend its range.

Everyone has probably read about the Passenger Pigeon of eastern

North America and its extinction. It is no compensation for the loss of this very distinct species that three old-world pigeons have been successfully introduced to the United States. Most widespread and abundant of these is the Feral Pigeon. In and around Los Angeles the Spotted Dove is now well established and thriving. It was first discovered there in 1917 and no one seems to know who introduced it or, if they do, wants to admit it. The Barbary Dove, a domesticated form of the African Collared Dove, is also found in Los Angeles but only in and around Sheridan Square, where it appears to be dependent on food given it by the public.

Parrots of many species have been imported into North America, as into other countries, as cage and aviary birds. Many escaped or liberated individuals of different species have survived for short periods but only one has shown signs of possibly succeeding in a feral state. This is the Quaker or Monk Parakeet, which is found naturally in the subtropical and temperate parts of South America. This noisy but otherwise attractive bird is a little smaller than a Feral Pigeon in size and stocky in build with a pointed tail. It is mainly soft green in colour with a pale grey face and breast, some blue on the wings and a pinkish-fawn bill. It inhabits open woodland, scrub, cultivated regions and orchards and sometimes causes damage to grain and fruit.

Nearly all other parrots breed in holes of trees, cliffs or buildings but Quaker Parakeets nest in the branches of trees. From two to twelve pairs build an enormous communal structure of sticks, each pair making and defending from the others their own individual nest hole in the mass of sticks.

John Bull (an *American* ornithologist, despite his name), writing in the *Wilson Bulletin* for December 1973, noted that 'within the past few years' this parakeet had established 'a sizeable resident population' in south-eastern New York and adjacent areas of Connecticut and New Jersey. There were, however, only a very few definite records of successful breeding and, as with feral parrots elsewhere, repeated escapes or liberations and the longevity of individuals might give a false idea of the species' success.

Probably action will be (or by the time this book appears already will have been) taken to suppress the Quaker Parakeets as official feeling in the U.S.A. seems now usually very much against the introduction of exotic species, other than those introduced for shooting purposes. As in Britain the sportsmen's enjoyment in shooting an exotic species is sometimes held to justify its introduction where aesthetic or sentimental pleasure in it would not. The Pheasant and the Common Partridge are examples; both were established long ago, and have met with considerable success so far. The Pheasant is the more successful, being now found over a fairly wide area from a little north of the Mason and Dixon line to northern New York State and parts of southern Canada, whereas the Partridge has been less successful and is most abundant in the upper Mississippi Valley. Although numbers of both species are bred in captivity each year and released for shooting purposes, it is almost certain that both would now hold their own even without this. The Chukar Partridge, a species very similar to the Red-legged Partridge but paler in colour, has been locally established in western North America in semi-arid, rocky country similar to that which it inhabits from the eastern Mediterranean regions to eastern Asia.

South America

The House Sparrow is widespread in southern South America. When I was in south-eastern Brazil in the autumn of 1972, I found it common in all inhabited areas that I visited. It appears to have been introduced by unknown persons, perhaps as a cage bird rather than with the deliberate intention of establishing it. Because of, rather than in spite of, the mental characteristics that make it so successful at living with man, the House Sparrow makes a very unsuitable cage or aviary bird unless it has been hand-reared. However, some bird-keepers always like to possess any bird that others do not have, regardless of its intrinsic merit. For this reason the House Sparrow has been carried about within South America, where bird-keeping and bird-dealing are widespread. It has now reached some places well to the north of its general range in the country and has been present in the new town Brasilia since 1959.

The Common Waxbill is found over much of Africa and is a favourite cage and aviary bird elsewhere. It was introduced before 1890 and became established in south-eastern Brazil. Through being carried about in the bird trade it has more recently colonised other eastern states – Mañaos on the Amazon, and, since 1964, Brasilia. The Common Waxbill is only found (so far) near towns, so presumably it cannot compete with native species in more natural environments. It has not yet been studied thoroughly in its new home, so it is impossible to say what conditions it needs there or why it, alone among the many African waxbills that must have been imported and often escaped, has been successful.

The Greenfinch is widespread on the south coast of Uruguay. The Goldfinch is a very recent introduction, so far found only in Uruguay in the provinces of Montevideo and Canelones. As there are many South American finches quite closely related to these two, it would be most interesting to have a comparative study of them and the native species of cardueline finches in their new home. I recommend this to any of my readers who may go to Uruguay and want to do some useful bird-watching in their spare time!

The Feral Pigeon is well established in many towns in southern South America, and is known to be living in the 'Rock Dove fashion' of its wild forebears on Masatierra Island in the Juan Fernandes Group. Mr Jeffery Boswall found it, in 1972, not only abundant in Buenos Aires, but high in the Andes at Abra Pampa, and in the southernmost town in the world, Ushuaia, in Tierra del Fuego.

The Californian Quail was introduced into Chile by 1870, probably with the deliberate intention of establishing it as a game-bird. It is now found over a considerable area in Chile and also on the Argentine side of the sierras in Cordoba and San Juan.

Relatively little has been written about introduced birds in this continent and for the information given here I am indebted to a German ornithologist, Helmut Sick, who lives in South America and who, besides making important studies on many native species, wrote a paper on the status of the introduced species in the *Bonner Zoologische Beiträge* for 1968.

Australia

I once read in a Victorian bird book a story about the first Skylark brought into a rough gold-mining district in old-time Australia. Word soon got around among the case-hardened but not, it would seem, unregenerate gold-miners that so-and-so had an *English Lark*. On the following Sunday all the homesick miners turned up in their best clothes to listen with tears in their eyes to the familiar song of their homeland. This, in some way not explained in the story, converted those who were atheists or agnostics to Christianity, and reconverted others who were lapsed Christians. It is certainly true that many of the early colonists in Australia wanted to see and hear Skylarks and other familiar birds nor were they long satisfied with hearing them sing inside cages, they soon started letting them out!

The House Sparrow was introduced in the middle of the last century and has, as might have been expected, thriven only too well. It is widespread in eastern and southern Australia and is common even in many small settlements 'miles away from anywhere' in the arid interior of South Australia. It did not, however, succeed in reaching Western Australia before public sentiment and official action turned against introduced creatures, and so when the odd Sparrow got into Western Australia, via the trans-continental railway or on shipboard, it was promptly shot. So far these efforts have been successful and Perth and other western towns are Sparrow-free. My guess, however, is that sooner or later the House Sparrow *will* succeed in establishing itself there.

The Tree Sparrow was also introduced into Australia and is now established in parts of Victoria and southern New South Wales. When I arrived at Melbourne Harbour in March 1965 I was astonished to see numbers of both Tree Sparrows and House Sparrows *inside* the big customs shed there. Next day while I was in a bank in the centre of the city I saw through the window some Tree Sparrows in one of the trees outside. I know of no other place where the House and Tree Sparrows live side by side in a town. Possibly the present situation is a temporary one and the Tree Sparrow will be displaced by its more pushful relative.

The Spotted Munia or Spice Bird is a rather sombre little Asiatic estrildid with dark reddish-brown head and upperparts, a golden tinge, but not a very bright one, on its upper tail coverts, a scale-like pattern in dark brown on its white underparts, and a thick greyish bill. In India and south-eastern Asia it is often kept as a cage bird and in that role is also exported in great numbers elsewhere. Indian bird dealers often dye it bright green, red or yellow prior to export. It is, or at least was, commonly kept in Australia as well as elsewhere and it is thought that the Spice Birds that first established themselves in eastern Australia around Sydney and Brisbane were the result of accidental escapes. I think it is much more likely they were a deliberate introduction by someone who, in view of the present laws against freeing foreign birds, kept silent about his activities. The species has now spread further north and is abundant in Townsville, where it seems partly to fill the role of the House Sparrow elsewhere and to have ousted by competition the prettier but apparently less adaptable native Australian estrildids.

The Goldfinch is established in south-eastern Australia. It is a bird of inhabited areas, living in and about parks, orchards and gardens, nesting in introduced trees and feeding on the seeds of dandelions, milk-thistles, thistles and other plants of its native land that have been also, but in their case unintentionally, introduced to Australia.

Until very recently the Goldfinch was also found in western Australia, about Perth and Albany. When I was in Nedlands, near Perth, in the autumn of 1965, I saw a few Goldfinches on most occasions when I went out in the neighbourhood and did not realise that in fact the bird was then already declining in numbers. I am indebted for details to correspondence with Dr Dom Serventy, who has prepared a paper on the subject which will almost certainly be published in *The West Australian Naturalist* before this book is in print, and to my friend Bob Stranger, a keen 'birdman' who lives in Perth.

It appears the Goldfinch was first noticed there at the Government Gardens, Perth, in October 1933, when it must have been (then) only recently introduced. It slowly spread into the suburbs and became completely established, though not particularly abundant, entered into a rapid decline from about 1963 and now appears to be extinct in and around Perth. Disease, lack of food due to much waste land having been built over, predation and trapping for the cage bird trade have all been suggested as possible reasons for the disappearance of the Goldfinch. Bob Stranger points out that these are likely to have been 'occupational risks' to the bird since its introduction and suggests another factor that he thinks might have been largely or even wholly responsible. This is the coincidental increase and urbanisation of the Singing Honeyeater in and around Perth. Although only about a third larger than a Goldfinch, this slender, greenish and greyish bird is extremely aggressive. It does not, as do most birds, restrict its attacks to nest predators, birds of the same species and other species that are obviously in competition with it but fiercely attacks all kinds of birds, especially those smaller and weaker than itself. It is known to eat the eggs of smaller birds and sometimes to cause their breeding to be unsuccessful by continually harrying the adult birds when they try to visit their nest.

Bob Stranger has witnessed attacks by Singing Honeyeaters on Goldfinches and, having myself seen the aggressive behaviour of this bird towards small native species in inland South Australia, I certainly do not think his theory implausible.

The Greenfinch is established in parts of Victoria, New South Wales and South Australia. It does not, however, seem, so far, to have spread far or to be very successful. As in England the Greenfinch appears a much more adaptable species than the Goldfinch it seems at first surprising that it has done less well in Australia. Possibly fewer of its European food plants have become established there but this is just a guess on my part and may be quite wrong. Certainly one plant whose seeds are eaten by it but not by the Goldfinch – the wild rose – is now common in eastern Australia.

The Blackbird was introduced to Melbourne about a hundred years or more ago and has prospered there ever since. It is also found elsewhere in south-eastern Australia and Tasmania, especially in and around Adelaide in South Australia. On my first bird-watching ramble in Australia, in Adelaide National Park in March 1965, it seemed to me 'all wrong' to see numerous Blackbirds in the same woodland as parakeets and Bronzewing Pigeons. The Blackbird, although very much a bird of gardens and parks in Australia, as in Europe, has also pushed out into fairly wild country in places. If this trend continues, as it is likely to, it will be interesting to see if the Blackbird will compete seriously with the native shrike-thrushes, birds which, although not related to true thrushes, are much like them in appearance and feeding habits.

The Song Thrush has, so far, become established only in and around the city of Melbourne. This species, although common in gardens and parks in England, has been much less successful in adapting to life alongside modern man than its relative the Blackbird in its native lands, and has also been less successful in the new countries to which man has introduced it.

The Starling has been highly successful in Australia as elsewhere. It is now one of the most abundant species in many parts of eastern Australia; in Victoria, South Australia, New South Wales and parts of Queensland; also in Tasmania. In general it is a bird of towns, hamlets, cultivated regions and farmlands. When in Australia I was, however, surprised at the dry and barren appearance of many of the fields or grazing lands in which great flocks of Starlings evidently managed to find food. In May 1965 I was wandering one morning along the banks of the Cooper River (then dry except for a few pools here and there) near Innamincka in the extreme north-east of South Australia. All about were (to me) exotic parakeets, pigeons, spoonbills, and a huge Black-backed Pelican had been swimming gravely on one tiny pool, when I suddenly noticed a bird in flight that had something familiar about it. It was alone, flying over the arid, drought-stricken open country beyond the river and making purposefully towards the 'timber' of the river bank. Yes, it was a Starling! Either a lone pioneer (I saw no others anywhere within hundreds of kilometres) or one that had mislaid its companions. Perhaps it was the first to arrive in the district, as I saw no others. In any case it appeared quite undaunted and, after a short rest in the branches, flew down and began to bathe at the edge of a pool with the bustling, self-confident air so characteristic of its species.

Another introduced species of starling is also doing well in Australia and Tasmania. This is the Common Myna or House Myna.

This bird plays much the same role in its native home – India and Ceylon – as the Starling does in Britain. It is, therefore, rather surprising that it and the Starling should *both* have been able (so far) to be so successful in Australia. The two species now overlap widely in parts of eastern Australia. Where they both occur the Myna does rather more scavenging in streets, gardens and garbage dumps while the Starling feeds more in the fields outside the towns and suburbs. The Myna's distribution is more patchy than that of the Starling but it extends further north in Queensland, and seems, as would be expected, to thrive better in the hot climate there than the Starling does. All the same the Myna is common in Melbourne, Tasmania and New Zealand, all places that are decidedly chilly at times.

The Red-eared Bulbul has become established in Sydney and, to a slight extent, in Melbourne. It is not known when or how its first representatives got to either place. This is a jaunty-looking bird, rather larger than a House Sparrow, with blackish head and forward curling crest, dark brownish upperparts, white cheeks and underparts, set off with a tuft of bright scarlet just behind the eye and scarlet under tail coverts. A native of India and south-east Asia, it is commonly kept as a cage bird in its native lands and exported in that capacity. Like other bulbuls it feeds on fruit and flowers as well as insects and has made itself unpopular thereby to gardeners and fruit growers.

The Spotted Dove has been introduced at various times to Australia and evidently from various places. In both Perth and Melbourne Spotted Doves resembling the race of the species found in the Malayan regions and much of south-east Asia (*S. chinensis tigrina*), which has more or less streaked wing-coverts, and others resembling the Chinese race (*S. c. chinensis*), which has almost uniformly brown wing-coverts, are both present and interbreed freely. This species is well established in towns and suburbs and is said to succeed even out in the 'bush' in some areas. It feeds on lawns, along roadsides, in gardens and cultivated fields and, at any rate around Perth, freely takes crumbs of bread and other scraps of human food.

In eastern Australia the Spotted Dove is the only 'turtledove', but in western Australia the African form of the Laughing Dove has also been introduced. Like the Starling and the House Myna these species seem in most parts of their natural range to have very similar habits to one another; both are typically species that live alongside man in towns, villages and cultivated regions. I had the impression that where they both were common the Spotted Dove tended to be more numerous in gardens and parks with many large, thickly-foliaged trees and the Laughing Dove in more open places with less tree cover. One of the main strongholds of both species was the Perth Zoo whence, it is said, they were first introduced to Western Australia in 1898. The Zoo grounds are (or at least were in 1965) not only a breeding area for innumerable pairs of each species but hundreds more came in from every direction to feed on the grain, bread and mash put down in open-topped pens for wallabies, pinioned water birds and other captives.

The Feral Pigeon has been successful in Australia as elsewhere. Whereas in most other places it depends upon buildings or cliffs for its nest sites, in parts of Australia it nests freely in the hollows of gum trees. Gum trees (*Eucalyptus*) of various species are the most abundant large trees over much of Australia. They tend to develop lots of very good holes in them (I speak as a bird-watcher not a forester, of course) and these holes are of all sizes, so that in most places the many hole-nesting Australian birds, from the tiny Chestnut-tailed Thornbill to the large cockatoos, have an ample choice of nesting sites. So, too, has the introduced Feral Pigeon and it is possible that in the future this habit may enable it to spread well away from towns and settlements, as parts of the arid interior of Australia have much in common with some arid regions in Africa and Asia which wild Rock Pigeons naturally inhabit.

New Zealand

In Australia most of the common birds in the towns are introduced species, but in New Zealand introduced European and Asiatic species predominate both in town *and* country, if we except some coastal regions and the fortunately still considerable areas of uninhabited forest. Of the species described as having succeeded in Australia, the House Sparrow, Goldfinch, Greenfinch, Skylark, Starling, House Myna, Song Thrush, Blackbird, Spotted Dove and Feral Pigeon are all also very well established in New Zealand. The two thrushes in particular have done even better for themselves than in Australia and have colonised both native forest and many offshore islands.

Other European species, most of which have not, so far as I know, been successfully introduced anywhere else have, however, succeeded in New Zealand. The Chaffinch is now one of the commonest and most widespread of New Zealand birds, having established itself in the natural forest well away from man and on the offshore and sub-antarctic islands as well as in inhabited country. Apart from a rather local (introduced) population in South Africa I know of no other instance of the Chaffinch succeeding in a new country, although this may partly be due to its not being such a popular favourite as, for example, the Goldfinch and hence much less often introduced.

The Redpoll has also thriven in New Zealand and established itself on most of the sub-antarctic islands. The race of Redpoll that breeds in England is a little smaller and darker in colour than the Mealy Redpoll of northern Europe which, in varying numbers, visits Britain in winter. As some of the New Zealand Redpolls are rather larger and paler than typical British breeding 'Lesser Redpolls' it is thought that the original stock, which was imported from Britain, consisted of both of these forms of the species.

The Yellow Bunting or Yellowhammer is widespread and common in all types of open country from alpine grassland to the sea coast. Another bunting, the Cirl Bunting, was also introduced with some degree of success for, just as this bird is rather rare and local in England, so it is likewise rather rare and local in New Zealand. The Cirl Bunting is primarily a bird of the Mediterranean region and it is probable that neither in England nor in New Zealand is the climate, in most districts, so favourable for it as for its relative.

The zeal with which the New Zealand colonists went about introducing British birds can be deduced from the fact that the sombre little Dunnock or Hedge Sparrow came within their scope. Possibly the person responsible had enjoyed birds-nesting as a boy and wanted his children also to have the thrill of discovering the Dunnock's beautiful rich blue eggs! The Dunnock belongs to a small family of birds (Prunellidae), whose headquarters are the Himalayan regions and most of whose species are hill and rock-haunting birds of high altitudes. Just as the Dunnock, the sole representative of its family in lowland Europe, is at home almost everywhere in Britain where there is some bushy cover, be it town park or cliffside scrub, so in New Zealand it thrives everywhere from sea level to mountains 1500 metres high so long as there is some fairly thick cover available.

Although crows are abundant in Australia, they do not occur naturally in New Zealand. This fact is, perhaps, less surprising than that the English colonists should have sought to make good the deficiency by introducing one. Predictably the crow they chose was the Rook, whose depredations were upon corn rather than Pheasants' eggs and which, in consequence, was not the object of such dislike as the Carrion and Hooded Crows. Also there is, to most of us, something essentially English-seeming about a Rookery and I have no doubt that homesickness for this typical feature of the British farmland was the *real* reason why Rooks were introduced, although no doubt a lot of dubious statistics about the numbers of harmful grubs and wireworms they could be expected to destroy were presented as the *good* reason for bringing them in.

Rooks are now established in a few places in both North and South Islands but one other colony was deliberately destroyed in the 1920s and recently one of the main colonies at Christchurch in South Island was greatly depleted by systematic poisoning of the birds. Ironically enough this was at the very place where the original stock was introduced. As in Britain, the Rook in New Zealand is typically a bird of arable farming country where cereals are grown.

The Australian Magpie or Piping-crow was imported freely into New Zealand in the last century and has done well in its new home. Naturally a bird that feeds much on the ground in more or less open country it has, both in New Zealand and in its native country, adapted itself easily to living in parks, cultivated areas and especially in areas of pastoral farming where grass fields are dotted or inter-spersed with clumps of shade trees. This handsome and sweet-voiced bird resembles the northern Magpie only in its (differently patterned) black and white colour. In general appearance it looks like a rather trim Crow or Rook with a large straight bill. Indeed some ornithol-ogists consider that the Piping-crow and its relatives the currawongs and (Australian) butcher-birds are fairly near relatives of the true crows. My own opinion is that, as passerine birds go, the true crows (Corvidae) and the piping-crows (Cracticidae) are not very close to each other. Both the Black-backed Magpie and the White-backed Magpie were introduced to New Zealand. It is a questionable point whether these are forms of the same species or whether the White-backed should be considered a distinct species (*G. hypoleuca*). The two certainly interbreed where their ranges overlap and are probably best treated as conspecific.

Piping-crows are almost omnivorous but much of their food con-sists of insects and other small creatures. Like the true crows they soon learn to eat all sorts of scraps of bread, cooked meat and other human foods. Those living in towns and suburbs often come regularly for handouts to bird-lovers' gardens. This readiness to lose fear of man can have one drawback. Such 'tame' Piping-crows, when they have eggs or young, sometimes attack people who, often quite un-wittingly, approach their nest. Their attacks can be painful even for adults and may be quite dangerous to small children. It is certainly not true, as the Magpie's defenders sometimes claim, that only birds-nesting children are attacked.

Attempts were, of course, made to introduce various game-birds into New Zealand. As elsewhere, the recent general change of opinion as to the desirability of introductions did not include the introduction of species considered suitable for shooting. Therefore fresh libera-tions of game-birds may constantly or occasionally occur to compli-cate the picture. The Pheasant and the Californian Quail are found in both North and South Island and are locally abundant. The Chukar Partridge is established in hilly country in the South Island. The Peafowl, Guineafowl and Turkey are also established in a few places in a feral state.

The Mallard was introduced mainly for shooting purposes but also as an ornamental bird for park waters. As might have been anticipated, it has succeeded only too well and not only is it now widespread but it has hybridised with the native Black Duck. This latter belongs to a group of very closely-related ducks which includes the common Mallard. Most of these species are geographically separated in a natural state, but where they are brought together in captivity or through ill-conceived introductions they usually breed together freely and produce fertile hybrids.

The Mute Swan, introduced from Britain, maintains itself on Lake Ellesmere and occurs in small numbers locally elsewhere. Its very differently-coloured relative the Australian Black Swan has done far better, and since its introduction shortly after the middle of the last century it has spread and is now a widely-distributed, abundant and thriving species.

I hope I will be forgiven if I digress here from the subject of introduced birds in New Zealand to mention the happy fact that at least one native bird, and that a rather spectacular one, shows every sign of becoming adapted to the changed conditions brought about by man. This is the New Zealand Pigeon. This is a fine, handsome bird, larger than the British Wood Pigeon, glossy green, deep purple and grey in colour with snow-white underparts that contrast beautifully with its green breast and red bill. A forest-dwelling species, it feeds on fruit, tender foliage and flowers and, like most pigeons, is considered good to eat by man. It was regularly trapped for food by the Maoris but at the time of the first white settlement of New Zealand was widespread throughout the forest areas.

Besides cutting down much of the forest, the white man (and of course those Maoris who obtained shot-guns too) shot the tasty pigeon extensively for food with the result that the bird soon began to decrease. Happily some restrictions on shooting of the New Zealand Pigeon were made law as early as 1864 and total protection granted to it in 1921. Since then the bird has made a come-back. It is now well established not only in forests but even in very small areas of residual forest. Moreover it now feeds on many introduced plants, taking the fruits of holly, rowan and cherry trees, the leaves and/or flowers of many other introduced trees and shrubs and even coming to the ground to eat clover.

It is probably a very fortunate thing that the only exotic pigeons introduced to New Zealand have been the Domestic Pigeon and the Spotted Dove, both of which are ground feeders. Had some versatile and partly tree-feeding species, such as the Wood Pigeon, been introduced and established in New Zealand it might possibly have prevented the New Zealand Pigeon from adapting itself to the new conditions as it seems to be in process of doing.

Europe

Whereas many introduced birds have been successful on some other continents, notably Australia and the Americas, very few have maintained themselves long in Europe. Probably this is mainly because the majority that have been tried were species whose natural environments are (for them) less harsh than the European one. Another hazard has undoubtedly been the dense human population of much of Europe and the wide dissemination of shot-guns among it. Even in Britain any birds that look unusual are still very liable to be shot in spite of public sentiment and the bird protection laws.

The Pheasant I shall deal with when discussing introductions to Britain. Other game-birds have flourished locally in Europe as a result of planned introductions but none seem to be fairly established. The magnificent Reeve's Pheasant seemed to have been successfully introduced in Austria. It throve and spread for many years, but has now died out. The Canada Goose has, however, become established in Scandinavia, as yet in rather small numbers and has, unlike its English relatives, re-evolved the habit of migrating south of the breeding range for the winter, as it does in its North American homeland.

Recently (1969) a delightful addition to the European avifauna has been discovered – the Common Waxbill. This tiny little estrildid is about the size of a Wren, brownish in colour with delicate faint barring, a red stripe from the bill to beyond the eye, a rosy red patch between the legs, and a dark brown tail that it switches from side to side when alarmed or excited. It feeds on seeds of grasses and tiny insects. It is found over a large part of southern and central Africa, south of the Sahara, and is imported in thousands into Europe as a cage and aviary bird. It has now been found established in Portugal, north of Lisbon, where it appears, from its numbers, to have been breeding successfully for some years.

It has been suggested that the population owes its origin to escapes from captivity but it seems more likely that somebody deliberately (and successfully) introduced it. It is unlikely that this delightful little bird will succeed far north of its present haunts though it might spread into parts of Spain. It might be mentioned that this is the species usually called St Helena Waxbill by bird dealers in England, though it is also an introduced species on St Helena.

Britain

Many people have tried to introduce foreign passerine birds but, so far, without any permanent success. The Pekin Robin, a beautiful and sprightly bird with grey, olive-green, orange and yellow plumage, touched with blue-black and red, has been tried repeatedly. Although a member of the babbler family (Timaliidae), it is rather Robin-like in shape and some of its movements and its large, dark eye. Small local populations have sometimes maintained themselves for years but have always died out sooner or later.

The American Robin has been introduced on several occasions. It ought, however, to have been obvious to anyone that a thrush whose way of life is the same as the endemic Blackbird's except that it is more highly migratory would be almost certain to fail in face of competition from the Blackbird, even if it did not come to grief in attempts to migrate. Although in some cases these introduced American Robins bred successfully at liberty in England nothing more was usually seen of them after the following winter. The occasional bird of this species that now turns up in England is invariably one that has crossed the Atlantic (probably an 'assisted passage' in most cases) or an escape from captivity.

Many species of parrots have been released or kept at liberty, again with no permanent success. Currently a few Rose-ringed Parakeets exist here and there in southern England but their persistence seems due to longevity rather than successful breeding. A group of 8, whose fortunes I endeavoured to follow, reared no young in 3 successive years, during which their numbers dwindled, and now (Jan. 1978) only 4 seem to be left.

Aviculturists have kept many species of foreign pigeons at liberty in this country, but in no case of which I am aware, have any managed to do more than maintain their numbers for a few years under such circumstances. In the early years of this century determined efforts were made, via the London Zoo, to introduce the Crested and Bronzewing Pigeons into Regent's Park. These two beautiful birds of the arid Australian 'bush' are surprisingly hardy in captivity in our cold, damp climate and it seems not to have been expected that they would succeed in establishing themselves beyond flying distance from the Zoo where they were to be regularly fed. As it was they did not even last long there.

The delightful Little Owl, immortalised as the bird of the Greek goddess Athene, was introduced into Britain in the latter part of the nineteenth century. Several landowners seem to have made some attempt but the two who did most and introduced large numbers of the species were Lord Lilford in Northamptonshire and E. G. B. Meade-Waldo in Kent. It is of interest that many introductions of this owl completely failed even though numbers were set free. In most of its range the Little Owl inhabits rather drier countries than Britain and it is probable that it spread north in Europe to such countries as Holland and Germany after agricultural man had destroyed much of the original forest.

In Britain it is at home in many types of open country where there are plenty of old trees or old buildings. It is usually thought, no doubt rightly, that the primary reason for its success is that it found a vacant niche in the avifauna, there being no other small owl. The only other small bird of prey that feeds mainly on insects and small mammals is the Kestrel. Its food is largely similar but it hunts by day and therefore tends to take different species of insects. It is true that the Little

Owl also hunts by day at times, as indeed do some other owls, but although it often perches more or less in the open by day it is *not* usually a day feeder, as some writers on birds have stated. I have yet to see a Little Owl hunting in full daylight although I have often seen Barn Owls doing so in winter, and when feeding young in the long summer days. The Little Owl seldom begins hunting until dusk. When I kept tame hand-reared owls as a boy I found my Tawny Owls (a species that seldom, if ever, hunts by day in a natural state) much more inclined to show hunting behaviour by day than were my Little Owls. This was no doubt because when young they had been fed at intervals throughout the day but not at night; that such conditioning should have less effect on the subsequent behaviour of the supposedly more diurnal Little Owls struck me even then as of interest.

The Little Owl's introduction took place at a time when the numbers of all birds of prey, including the Kestrel, had been greatly reduced by intensive game-preservation. Probably this lack of poss-ible part-competitors (both for food and for nesting sites) was of help to the Little Owl when getting established. Needless to say it soon became an object of the game-preserver's enmity itself. To the usual zeal for destroying any bird or beast that might possibly take a Par-tridge or Pheasant chick was added denunciation of the bird as an unwelcome foreigner and, to enlist the sentimental small-bird lovers against it as well, it was represented as a threat to Britain's song birds into the bargain. An inquiry into its feeding habits was undertaken by the British Trust for Ornithology in the 1930s. This showed that the greater part of its food (about 95 per cent) consisted of insects and small mammals. This report was, and often still is, denounced by many sportsmen as 'whitewashing by the paper naturalists' and does not, of course, have any effect on the treatment meted out by them to the Little Owl. In spite of persecution it throve, however, and when I was a boy in the 1930s it was much the commonest owl in those parts of Surrey and Middlesex known to me. Now, although not exactly rare, it seems everywhere to have decreased. Whether this is the result of persecution, poisoning (via its prey) with insecticides, the effect of our weather (which in the past twenty-five years or so has tended to be colder), the destruction of so many old, hole-providing field and hedgerow trees, or a combination of these and/or other factors, is not yet known.

The Pheasant was for a long time thought to have been introduced into Britain by the Romans, who certainly kept it in captivity at home in Italy and may well have done so in their colonies too. Supposed Pheasant bones having on re-examination turned out to be those of Domestic Fowls, and the earliest *preserved* written mention of Pheasants in Britain being in the Waltham Abbey Ordnance, it is now usually said to have been introduced shortly before the Norman Conquest.

Certainly the Pheasant is a striking-looking and highly edible bird and if it had been widespread and common would probably have appeared previously in some recorded writing. Also the form of Pheasant originally occurring in Britain and some other parts of Europe is said to have been identical with that found on the west coast of the Caspian Sea and the valleys and northern slopes of the Caucasus. I have not, however, seen evidence that any specimens of Pheasants from Britain that date back to before the *known* introduction of Pheasants from other lands have been compared critically with specimens from the Caucasus. My own opinion is that although the Pheasant may have been introduced by the Anglo-Saxons or others in early times the evidence is not fully convincing and it is just possible that it was a native of Britain albeit a rather rare or local one.

Be this as it may, the 'Old English Black-necked Pheasant,' so far as we know inseparable from the Caucasian race *Phasianus c. colchicus*, has been with us since at least before 1066. Early in the eighteenth century some landowners began to introduce a Chinese race of the species (*Phasianus c. torquatus*), a paler bird in which the male has a greenish-blue rump, mainly golden upperparts, and a broad white ring dividing the green of his upper neck from the gold and bronze of his back and breast. Many other races have since been introduced, including the Green or Japanese Pheasant (*Phasianus c. versicolor*), which some authorities consider a distinct species and in which the male is dark green on breast and underparts, and the large coppery form from parts of Manchuria and Mongolia (*Phasianus c. mongolicus*) which is as dark as the British original bird but has a very broad white collar. As a result the modern British Pheasants are mostly racial mongrels, although often beautiful ones, and, except in areas where some landowner or sporting syndicate is trying to 'improve' the stock by turning down large numbers of Pheasants of pure or allegedly pure race, one will hardly find two cock Pheasants that look exactly alike. More often than not, however, they show some trace of the white collar of the ring-necked eastern races.

An interesting colour variety of the Pheasant first appeared in England and has since occurred elsewhere in Europe. In this 'melanistic mutant', as it is usually called, the cocks are more or less dark, glossy blackish-green and dark purple all over and the hens are much darker than most hen Pheasants, being of a general dark chocolate colour (but, like normal individuals, with a complicated pattern of markings) very similar to a hen Red Grouse. The chicks of these dark Pheasants are chocolate or blackish with white patches on their heads, unlike the cryptically patterned brown, buff and black normal chicks. Some people think that this dark variety arose from crossing with the Green Pheasant but this is most unlikely. In the first place the hen of the Green Pheasant is very similar to those of other Pheasants and quite unlike the dark brown hen of the melanistic form. Secondly, this melanistic form of the Pheasant is in many respects similar to dark varieties of other game-birds, such as the 'Japanese' Peafowl and the Dark Golden Pheasant, that have appeared spontaneously among captive stock. Probably such dark freaks have often occurred among wild populations of Pheasants in different parts of the world but never become established owing to their greater conspicuousness, especially when chicks, causing proportionately more of them to get killed by predators. In some parts of Britain, probably because the Pheasant's natural enemies, man excepted, are mostly killed off, the dark form is evidently under no disadvantage and so has managed to thrive. There is indeed some circumstantial evidence to suggest that these dark varieties may be hardier and stronger than normally coloured birds and have selective advantage over them under the rather unnatural conditions of the aviary or game preserve.

The Pheasant is often wrongly spoken of as 'pampered' by those who disapprove of game-preserving; it is in fact a very tough and viable bird and the oft-repeated statement that it would 'die out' but for game-preservation is almost certainly untrue. Or perhaps I had better say it is only true of those areas, and they are all too many, where it is in fact, if not in theory, persecuted by man in season and out. So long as man does not prey too heavily on it the wild, or feral, Pheasant manages to maintain its numbers in many areas. It likes plenty of cover and although often in quite dry woods shows some preference for low-lying, rather wet woods, the tangled scrub along stream banks, reedbeds and similar places. However, it feeds a lot in fields, glades in woods and other open areas and can often make do with surprisingly little cover. It is omnivorous, taking largely vegetable food such as seeds, shoots, and buds of many plants, chestnuts, acorns, and berries. It also takes some insects and the young chicks feed chiefly on insects at first although they quite soon begin to take some vegetable food.

In the few places where it is not shot at the Pheasant soon becomes relatively indifferent to people, if it constantly sees them, and then becomes a living ornament whose beauty can be appreciated by the ordinary passer-by as well as by the bird-watcher with binoculars. I seldom see a cock Pheasant, shining in the sun, without thinking of the ancient Greek philosopher, Solon, who, when asked by the vainglorious Persian king if he (Solon) had ever seen anything so magnificent as himself and his court replied that, having seen the beauty of the Pheasant, he could no longer be impressed by mere human finery.

Other species of pheasants have been introduced and have thriven for a time here and there, usually only in places where they have been carefully protected from man, the most formidable predator on game-birds in Britain and, indeed, throughout the world. At the present time there are localities where feral populations of the brilliant Golden Pheasant and one or two where its equally beautiful relative the Amherst Pheasant are breeding in a feral state. In recent years the Golden Pheasant has increased and an attempt to exterminate the Amherst failed. Whether either species will ever be able to increase to significant numbers, spread and eventually rejoice the eyes of the casual hiker in our countryside remains to be seen. I think it is unlikely, but I hope I am wrong in this opinion. They are generally disliked by sportsmen and, owing to their weak flight and tendency to rely on running, or hiding, any *well*-organised effort to get rid of them would be likely to succeed.

The Red-legged Partridge, now a fairly common bird in much of southern and eastern England, is unusual in being an example of a wild species that has been successfully introduced well to the north of its natural range. Naturally it is found only in south-western Europe and is replaced by allied species in the eastern Mediterranean, Asia and north Africa. The successful introduction of the Red-leg seems to have started in the late eighteenth century in Suffolk and subsequently elsewhere. Once it succeeded in establishing itself it was not long before some people wished to get rid of it. Because it is rather more inclined than the Common Partridge to start running away from man at distance, instead of crouching in alarm till he gets really near and then taking wing, the Red-leg was less easily shot in numbers when it was the fashion to 'walk up' partridges. This made some sportsmen look on it with disfavour and since sportsmen, like most of us, are ever ready not only to believe any sort of accusation against anybody or anything they dislike but also, very often, to invent false accusations, it was not long before the 'Frenchman', as its detractors termed it, was being accused of all sorts of unlikely 'crimes'. It was said to fight and drive away Common Partridges and even to hunt down and kill their chicks. There seems to have been no evidence for these statements – the two species usually ignore one another. Modern sportsmen, less energetic than their forebears, usually prefer to have their partridges driven up to and over them by beaters and since the Red-legged Partridge is just as vulnerable as the Common to this method of shooting it is no longer looked on with such disfavour.

Although in England the Red-legged and Common Partridges often occur in the same places, the former is more particularly a bird of rather dry, sparsely grown habitats such as stony or chalky upland fields, coastal dunes, and, very often, of the rough waste and weed-grown land in and around gravel pits, cement works or derelict farms. In its native haunts in southern France and Spain it is also found both in wild and cultivated country that is usually rather arid. It is interesting to speculate on the reasons for its success in a more northerly climate. First in importance is, of course, the fact that man had created more or less open habitats similar to some of those it lived in 'back home'. Secondly, and I think this may also have been of considerable importance, predators were less numerous. In its native countries the Red-leg had not only been intensively hunted by man – with guns, traps and nets – for hundreds, perhaps (guns excepted) for thousands of years, but it also had to contend with a great number of birds and beasts of prey. In England not only was the human persecution probably less intense, even during the periods when the Red-leg was being killed off as 'vermin', but the birds and beasts of prey, fewer in species anyway than in Spain or southern France, had been reduced to very low numbers by man, especially in those dry eastern counties most suitable for the Red-leg.

In the past few years actions have been taken which might have a great, and in my opinion unwelcome effect on the British Red-legged Partridges. The closely-related Chukar Partridge, which I have already mentioned as having been successfully introduced to parts of the United States, has now been introduced into England. These introductions appear so far to have been chiefly in the eastern counties (the stronghold of the British Red-legs!) but also locally elsewhere. In 1975 I saw a pair on the embankment when I looked out of a train window in Hampshire. Hybrids between the two species, which interbreed where they have been brought into contact with each other by human agency, have also been introduced.

The alleged reasons for introducing Chukar Partridges and their hybrids is that they are better 'sporting' birds or are believed by their sponsors to be so. Whether this is so or not, it seems beyond doubt that Chukar Partridges are easier, or perhaps one should say even easier, to keep and reproduce in captivity than is the Red-leg. It is early yet to do more than guess at what the results of introducing the Chukar to Britain will be but, especially if further introductions take place as it seems likely they will, one of two things seems likely to happen. Either competition with the Chukar will eventually eliminate the Red-legged Partridge from some or all of its English habitats or else extensive hybridisation and consequent loss of pure Red-legged stock will result. The latter has, I am told, already occurred in parts of the Red-leg's native countries where there has been deliberate introduction of large numbers of Chukars.

Replacement of Britain's Red-legged Partridges by Chukar Partridges or hybrids might please sportsmen by providing more, and marginally bigger, partridges to shoot but from other points of view seems to me a sorry prospect. Both species, at least in their pure state (I have not yet seen hybrids myself), are beautiful birds. I think the Red-leg the more beautiful but that is perhaps a personal bias. The Chukar, however, besides being so easy to breed in captivity, has not only a very wide natural range – being found from south-eastern Europe through much of the Middle East eastward to China and Mongolia – but is also well established as an introduction in both North America and New Zealand. The Red-legged Partridge, on the other hand, is native only to south-western Europe (where its range is known to have contracted within historic times) and, apart from England, has only been successfully introduced to some of the Atlantic islands. Moreover, in at least some of its natural range, introduction of the Chukar Partridge has already taken place.

The keeping of waterfowl – ducks, geese and swans – has long been widely practised in Britain. There is no public feeling against the keeping of wild waterfowl in captivity as there is against the keeping of most other wild birds. There are, I think, two main reasons for this; first, because waterfowl have been and are kept to a large extent by rich and influential people and organisations whom those agitating against the keeping of other kinds of wild birds have not, for obvious reasons, wished to antagonise; and second, because it is common custom not to keep waterfowl in aviaries but to cut off the end joint of a wing so as to render them permanently flightless and then turn them loose on ornamental waters, where they appear 'free' to naive observers.

It is fairly certain in some cases, and probable in others, that the present-day breeding distribution of some of the native ducks within

Britain has been influenced by the deliberate liberation or accidental escape of captive birds: the Gadwall that breed in London are an obvious example. In all such instances, however, the picture is confused because even if the original stock in a particular area owes its origin to human interference their presence may have caused genuine wild individuals to settle there with them. Also many small and usually short-lived colonies of truly foreign species have been established or have established themselves through the straying of the full-winged young of captive parents. Some such groups are still in existence but seem very much dependent on the 'grace and favour' of local landowners. Two foreign species seem, at present, to be fairly firmly established. These are the Canada Goose and the Mandarin Duck; possibly the Egyptian Goose, and the Ruddy Duck, also now come into this category.

The Canada Goose was first introduced in the eighteenth century. It was kept as a park ornament and is still today very largely based on parks and country estates where it enjoys some measure of protection by man, *from* man. In the last few decades some estate owners have become more concerned than formerly with the profit from farms within or without their boundaries. As a result they have sometimes taken action against the flocks of Canada Geese that they formerly protected, as these birds, being feeders on grass and other herbage, can do a fair amount of damage on fields of young wheat and other grains. Often the problem has been solved bloodlessly, however, by giving the birds away to others, especially to municipal authorities, some of whom, no matter how crowded their park waters with pinioned rarer waterfowl which can ill brook competition for space and handouts of food from the public, seem unable to say 'no' when offered 'owt for nowt'.

The Mandarin Drake is one of the most spectacular birds in the world. It combines rich and bright though in no way gaudy colouring with a very unusual shape, due to the enormously enlarged inner web of the innermost secondary of each wing. These stand up like little sails when the bird is at ease or (still more) when it is displaying. The natural home of the Mandarin is in the Far East. It is a bird of wooded streams and pools, particularly oak woods, as acorns are, when it can get them, one of its chief foods. It has now become rare or extinct over large parts of its former range due partly to human persecution but mainly to the destruction of the forests which provided it with food and nesting sites, as, like many other ducks, it nests in holes in trees.

I was nine years old when I first saw feral Mandarins, although it was not until some years later that I fully believed that I had done so. It happened, oddly enough, only a few days after I had, for the first time in my life, seen a coloured picture of the species. I was wandering along near the Bourne, a little stream that ran between rather high and thickly tree-fringed banks through the fields some way behind our house at Virginia Water in southern England. I ran suddenly down through an opening in the vegetation to the stream's edge: right in front of me on a sand-bar stood a little group of Mandarins. Just how many I never knew, probably four as I clearly saw two drakes – and I can see them in mind's eye to this day nearly 50 years later – as for a split second they stood, frozen with fear at my sudden appearance. Then they leapt into the air and were gone. I literally did not believe my own eyes for I knew that Mandarin Ducks *could not* be there and also I knew that the picture in the book had made a strong impression on me. Later I often puzzled over the matter and came to the 'rational' conclusion that I must have briefly glimpsed some brightly-coloured British ducks, such as Shovellers, and my imagination, still full of the picture of Mandarins, had turned them into this species. It was an interesting example of how, when we try to be reasonable and objective, we often end up with a completely false idea of situations where we would have done better had we trusted our feelings or our eyes.

Later I often saw smallish ducks with conspicuous white bellies flying in little parties or pairs in the half light on cold winter evenings and, being then rather ignorant of wildfowl, thought they must be Wigeon. It was not until 1938 that I discovered that the Mandarin Duck was, by that time, quite common in the district, with its headquarters in Windsor Park, and that my white-bellied ducks that flew so swiftly through the woods at dusk were of this species.

The Mandarin Duck now occurs locally in a few parts of Britain.

The most thriving colony at the moment would appear to be in Surrey and adjacent areas of Berkshire where it is fairly common in and around Windsor Great Park, and small numbers can be seen as far away from the main 'headquarters' as Leatherhead. Woking and Reading. The Mandarin needs wooded country with tree-fringed lakes, pools or streams. It must have trees that supply suitable hollows for nesting and although it will, at a pinch, nest at some distance from water, in doing so it greatly decreases its chances of getting the ducklings safely from the nest to a suitable rearing area. Like many other ducks the Mandarin readily learns to become tame and accept artificial food where it sees many humans who offer bread rather than lead. I have seen still flightless young Mandarins, on a pond near Epsom, that would come up on the bank and take food at people's feet, although their mother was more wary and kept at a little distance. Such young are, unfortunately, not likely to survive long if they later move to areas where ducks are shot.

The successful introduction into Britain of this harmless, beautiful and threatened species is, in my opinion, to be welcomed on both aesthetic and conservational grounds. Those who object to all introductions on the ground that man should not interfere with nature have my sympathies but they might bear in mind that some of our native species would not be here but for man's past and continued interferences. Such officially approved introductions as exotic coniferous trees, which replace previously existing woodlands, farmlands and moors, and the Rainbow Trout, to aid in whose establishment the native species of fishes in many waters are deliberately destroyed, are far more likely to have adverse effects on our native wildlife and are, therefore, far more worthy objects of their opposition.

Hawaii

Hawaii has suffered more than most countries from over-zealous attempts to introduce foreign birds. As late as 1936 a 'buy a bird' campaign, for the introduction of more exotic species, was in full swing. The results have been disastrous to some of the native birds, as there is considerable evidence to suggest that the extinction of some species and the decline of others has been due to the spread of diseases, particularly avian malaria, carried by introduced species and spread by mosquitoes. The mosquitoes themselves were also introduced, through carelessness in cleaning out ships' water casks.

The majority of the birds that were introduced failed to establish themselves although the number that did so was greater than in other places, New Zealand perhaps excepted. Only some of the more successful introductions will be mentioned here. Readers especially interested in the introduced birds of Hawaii should consult past and current issues of *The Elepaio*, Hawaii's excellent ornithological journal which makes fascinating reading.

The Skylark is established widely on three of the Hawaiian islands (Niihau, Maui and Hawaii) and occurs also on four others. The Hwamei or Spectacled Laughing-thrush is common on Kauai and occurs locally on Oahu, Hawaii, Molokai and Maui. It is a rather thrush-like bird that belongs to the babbler family (Timaliidae), of a rich reddish-brown colour with a white spectacle-like marking around its eye. It has many pleasing whistling notes and is a favourite cage bird of the Chinese, so it is possible that the Hawaiian stock originated from escapes rather than from deliberate release of birds.

A second bird of the same family is the beautiful and lively Pekin Robin, which has been mentioned in connection with the many unsuccessful attempts to establish it in Britain (p. 124). In Hawaii it has thriven and is found abundantly on the islands of Oahu, Maui and Hawaii, wherever there is plenty of low bushy or brushy cover.

Another south Asian species, the Shama, is established locally on Kauai and Oahu in areas where there are thickets or forests with undergrowth. This is a bird of the thrush family (Turdidae), rather larger than the British Robin in size but with a long tail, and black in colour with chestnut belly and white rump. It has a melodious song and has long been a favourite cage bird. Locally on Oahu its close relative the black and white Magpie-robin, whose English name well describes it, is also naturalised.

The House Myna, already discussed in reference to its successes in Australia and South Africa, is found on all the main Hawaiian islands and is common in both towns and cultivated regions although only found locally and in small numbers in forest.

The Japanese White-eye is a little dull green and brownish bird, with a conspicuous white ring of plush-like feathers round its eye, and a pale yellow throat. The white-eyes, most of whose many species are very similar in general appearance and which belong to a family of their own, are warbler-like birds which feed on insects, soft fruits and nectar and are usually numerous wherever they occur. The present species has been highly successful in its new home and occurs on all main islands wherever there are trees or bushes in quantity.

The House Sparrow has, unfortunately, been as successful here as elsewhere and is firmly established. So too, interestingly enough, is another predominantly seed-eating species that might have been thought unlikely to be able to establish itself in competition with the Sparrow. This is the House Finch, previously mentioned as having been introduced to Long Island, New York, from Mexico and parts of western North America. It is a dull streaky brown bird, the male enlivened with bright red forehead, 'eyebrows', breast and rump. In its native lands it often lives around human dwellings although also found in uninhabited country.

The House Finch is one of the many birds with red plumage which in captivity usually lose their red colour, the red feathers being replaced by feathers of some shade of yellowish or gold. It is of some interest that a large proportion of the Hawaiian population of this species show a possibly comparable although less extreme change of colour, having the bright parts of the plumage yellow, golden or orange instead of red.

The Cardinal of North and Central America is well established on all the main Hawaiian islands. It is a striking bird, nearly as large as a Song Thrush and rather slender in build with longish tail, crested head and thick bill. The male is mainly bright or darkish red in colour (there is some geographical and also individual variation) with a black face mask and brownish-red back, wings and tail; the female is mainly brownish. It is a bird of the wood edge, thickets and riverside trees but has taken to living also in gardens and parks and become an habitual and favourite 'bird-table bird' both in its native U.S.A. and in Hawaii.

Despite its name the Red-crested Cardinal is not particularly closely related to the previous species, although also now thought, like the Cardinal, to be more closely related to the buntings than to the true finches. It is about the same size, grey and white in colour with a vivid scarlet head and crest. The sexes are alike in plumage but young birds are at first browner and have reddish-brown heads and crests. It occurs naturally in South America, in southern Brazil, Paraguay, Uruguay and northern Argentina. It feeds mainly on seeds and insects but in many places has learnt to scavenge scraps of human food about habitations. In Hawaii it is common on Oahu and is also found locally on Kauai and Maui.

Both the Feral Pigeon and the Spotted Dove, already discussed in reference to their successes elsewhere, are firmly established. So also is the little Barred Ground Dove or Zebra Dove. This is a small, long-tailed dove with blackish barring over most of its light brownish-grey plumage, a pinkish central stripe on its breast and white-tipped outer tail feathers that are conspicuous when it fans and raises its tail in display. It is found in the Malayan regions (with rather distinct subspecies in Australasia) where it is very commonly kept in captivity. It feeds mainly on seeds picked up from the ground and nests in bushes and trees. It has done well in Hawaii where it occurs chiefly in agricultural land and around human habitations.

Feral Chickens, that had largely reverted to the habits and way of life of the ancestral Red Jungle Fowl, were formerly found on all the main islands, no doubt as a result of domestic birds having strayed or been lost. They probably owed their origin to chickens kept by the early Polynesians rather than to those of later European and Asiatic invaders. They are now said to be found only on Kauai and locally on Niihau. Their extinction elsewhere seems most likely to be due to human persecution.

Later and deliberate attempts to establish stocks of other game-birds had considerable success. Feral Peafowl, one of the largest and certainly the most spectacular of all game-birds, are to be found, albeit in restricted areas, on Oahu, Kauai, Niihau, Molokai, Maui and Hawaii. Other game-birds of which there are now thriving feral populations in the Hawaiian islands are the Chukar Partridge, Pheasant and Californian Quail. Both the ring-necked and green races of the Pheasant (or species, for as has been said previously, some authorities consider the green Japanese form a separate species) occur. Although they interbreed in Hawaii the Green Pheasant is said to be more a bird of open forest and less of cultivated regions than the Ring-necked Pheasant, and to occur in pure form on the moist windward slopes of Mauna Kea and Mauna Loa.

Quails of the genus *Coturnix* have also been successfully established here and there in grass country and farmland. Mostly, and perhaps entirely, they derive from Japanese Quail, a species widely spread in the Far East and domesticated as an egg and food producer in Japan. In a wild state it is migratory over much of its range; so it would be interesting to know whether the successful introductions were of non-migratory populations or domestic birds in which the migratory instinct had degenerated. The persistent failure of attempts to introduce the European Quail elsewhere have usually, and probably correctly, been ascribed to its coming to grief through attempts to migrate. The Australian Pectoral Quail was also introduced and is said to occur on Niihau, and possibly to have interbred with Japanese Quail elsewhere.

Comments on introductions

People sometimes imagine that it is usually very easy for foreign birds to get a foothold in a new country and overrun it in no time at all. Probably this is because in a justifiable reaction against the previous century's zeal for introducing or trying to introduce foreign birds and other animals, the dangers of chance escapes are sometimes overestimated. So far as birds are concerned (the situation may be very different with some plants and insects) the evidence suggests that in most, and perhaps all cases, even the most successful (or perhaps, with hindsight, we might now say unsuccessful) introductions did not succeed until at least a dozen or more individuals were freed. Sometimes, as with the Starling in America and the Red-legged Partridge in England, it required two or more such introductions in different years before success was finally achieved.

Introduced species can sometimes establish themselves, if they find a vacant or only partially filled ecological niche in their new home. Sometimes, however, particularly on islands, which often have a rather impoverished avifauna, they may succeed even in partial competition with native species if they find an otherwise similar, but in some way less exacting, environment to that to which they were adapted at home. Commonly, when man has introduced a species of bird·which has successfully established itself, he had previously created an environment essentially similar to that which it was already adapted to.

All species which have had great success as introductions, and have thereby become well established, widespread, and abundant not only on small islands but also on large islands and/or continents, are species that were already very abundant, widespread, and thoroughly used to living alongside man in their homelands. The Starling, House Sparrow, Feral Pigeon and Mallard are obvious examples.

Those introductions that have, viewed from the point of view of the species itself and those wholeheartedly in favour of its introduction, been highly successful commonly involve birds that were introduced to parts of the world where no other birds of their family occurred naturally. The Starling and House Sparrow in North America, Australia and New Zealand; Yellow Buntings, Chaffinches, Redpolls, Blackbirds and Dunnocks in New Zealand; and all the thriving introduced species in Hawaii are obvious examples. Many less outstanding successes, such as the Rook in New Zealand and the Common Waxbill in Portugal and Brazil, come, of course, into the same category.

There are, however, also birds that have had high or moderate success when introduced to countries where their families were already represented among the native birds but not by any species very closely related to them and/or with very similar habits and consequent needs. Examples of this are the Feral Pigeon in the Americas and Australia, the Pheasant in North America, the Red-legged Partridge in Britain, the Little Owl in Britain and New Zealand and the Spotted Munia in eastern Australia.

The only instances I can think of where introduced species have been successful in spite of the presence of closely-allied native species are the following: The Feral Pigeon is highly successful in some parts of central Asia and eastern Asia, in spite of the presence of the very closely-related Eastern Rock Pigeon or Blue Hill Pigeon. In the main, as might have been expected from its domesticated ancestry, the Feral Pigeon seems more successful in and around towns and the Eastern Rock Pigeon in more natural habitats but there is considerable overlap. A study of their comparative ecology where both occur, as in Ulan Bator, the capital of Mongolia, would be of great interest but has yet to be made. The House Sparrow has been successful in South Africa in spite of native birds of the same genus, none of which, however, was adapted to living alongside man. In some other parts of

the world, incidentally, the House Sparrow has extended its range in its role of camp follower of agricultural or technological man, successfully excluding or ousting related species of sparrows from the 'house sparrow' niche in so doing. The Mallard has been a moderate success in New Zealand and Australia in spite of the presence of the closely-related native Black Duck, with which it hybridises. The present evidence suggests again that the Mallard (and hybrids favouring it in their characters) is more successful in town parks and other artificial habitats but (so far) less so in remaining natural habitats than the Black Duck.

CHAPTER FIVE

BIRDS AND BREAD

As will have become clear from much in some preceding chapters, a great many individuals of various bird species have learnt to eat white bread and similar substances, and supplement their diet with it to varying degrees. In those populations of many species which live in towns or suburbs, such food may be a major part of the diet throughout the year; as with many Mute Swans, Feral Pigeons and House Sparrows, for example. With others, it may be a mainstay only in times of shortage of other foods, or only of significance in periods of exceptionally adverse weather. Leaving aside such aspects as nutrition and digestion – except to say that whether or not it has been beneficial to man, the enrichment of white bread with added vitamins and minerals appear to have virtually ended the occurrence of beri-beri in London's Feral Pigeons – feeding on bread and similar substances poses some intriguing questions. Among these are how bread is recognised as food, since it does not resemble in appearance or texture any of the natural foods of most birds; to what extent and how the species feeding on bread compete or avoid competition with each other; and the effects of the bread supply on individual or specific success.

I shall here discuss these subjects in relation to some British species. My observations have been largely made in London and its suburbs. The taking by birds of foods supplied by man but of a more 'natural' character, such as seeds, nuts, fish, mealworms and meat, will not be dealt with except in reference to bread-eating. The list of species is not meant to include all birds that eat bread, but only those species many of whose members habitually do so, and which have often been watched when so doing. The term 'bread' is used to include other essentially bread-like foods, such as cake, pastry, buns, scones and biscuits.

Recognition

Many birds learn to eat bread through the example of their parents or other experienced individuals. The inexperienced bird watches an experienced individual feeding, sees what it is eating and soon starts to eat the same food – in some cases (as can be readily seen with the Feral Pigeon) not so quickly as it does when the mentor is feeding on natural foods. In species such as the Coot and Blackbird, in which the parents present their offspring with food held in the bill, the young will often have learnt the appearance and edibility of bread even before they become independent.

Birds of species that habitually try to rob others of food, such as the Blackbird and most gulls, appear to understand (whether innately, intuitively, or through learning is uncertain) that anything another bird is eating, trying to eat or carrying in the bill is likely to be edible. Such species probably often learn to eat bread, and other new foods, in the course of their robberies.

Initially, however, some individual birds must have learnt to eat bread without parental or other example; this must still happen when man and bread appear in hitherto uninhabited country. During the last war, for example, many Crested Larks and Lesser Short-toed Larks in eastern Libya learnt to eat army biscuit.

In many cases the initial eating of bread probably starts with normal foraging behaviour; such birds as crows and tits habitually investigate many kinds of novel objects and appear by doing so to learn many new foods and food sources. Others which are less catholic in diet nevertheless tend to peck at any small objects about the size of the seeds or other foods that they normally eat. It appears to be only species which normally take some immobile foods, such as seeds, vegetation, pupae or other immobile insects, or carrion, which learn to eat bread and similar foods in a wild state. Species such as most swallows and some flycatchers, that take only moving prey, seldom or never do so.

In some cases the investigation and subsequent eating of bread may originate as a side-effect of the search for minerals. Many birds, when in need of calcium (and possibly of other minerals), peck at and attempt to eat any white or whitish objects. It seems quite likely that bread is sometimes first sampled for this reason, and is discovered to be a palatable source of food even though not, to any appreciable extent, of the mineral(s) whose need first caused the bird to investigate it.

Feeding behaviour and competition

Some natural foods are eaten by as many species as is bread, but I cannot think of one in Britain (in the tropics termites might qualify) that is eaten as a staple food or as an important stop-gap in time of dearth, by so diverse a variety of species. As bread, and other foods given by humans or discarded by them, tends, like such natural foods as ripe fruits but to a greater degree, to be available in strictly limited areas, competition is to be expected, and does in fact occur. Some species are probably prevented from taking bread to the extent that they otherwise would because of competition from others. Many species are restricted by their feeding behaviour, which has evolved in relation to natural situations. Such natural differences of feeding methods enable some species to avoid or limit competition even when taking the same food. I shall now describe some bread-eating species in detail.

Mute Swan

In and near towns Mute Swans feed largely on bread and a majority of those living in well-populated parts of the countryside have also learnt to eat it, and to recognise humans as potential food givers. As swans naturally feed largely by grubbing about for sub-aquatic plants and their roots it is possible that the taste of their foods plays as great a part as appearance and may have originally led to bread-eating, although the majority nowadays probably learn by parental example.

The Mute Swan is restricted in its feeding to the waters where it lives and their immediate vicinity. Its use of bread is, therefore, limited to food deliberately given to it on or near the water; and to the spillage from garbage barges into rivers or other waters. Its feeding movements, evolved for an unhurried pulling and shaking free of vegetation or sub-aquatic roots, are ill-adapted for breaking up bread on land and not very quick or efficient at doing so even in the water. Mute Swans seem to have much more difficulty in swallowing pieces of bread, unless these are well saturated or relatively small, than do most ducks and geese.

Leaving aside the effects of its well-known aggressiveness towards other waterfowl that approach it in size and form such as Canada Geese, or in having white or partly white plumage like the Shelduck (*Tadorna tadorna*) and some domestic ducks, and considering only its role as food competitor, the Mute Swan probably has only a locally depressing effect on the bread-eating of other water birds, particularly surface-feeding ducks.

Mallard

This duck is more or less tame, and feeds largely on bread, in many town and suburban parks, on rivers flowing through towns or suburbs and on some public waters in country districts. It is probable that, but for its widespread persecution by shooters, it would, like the Mute Swan, have become fairly tame almost everywhere. It may often 'discover' bread by experiment as some natural foods seem to be largely found by touch or taste, but the example of experienced individuals is probably now a major factor in most cases.

Although the Mallard, like the Mute Swan, usually only feeds on bread available on or in the immediate vicinity of water, it is a much more agile bird. When in competition with others it moves quickly whether on land or in water, it can both strain tiny crumbs of bread from water and make away with large crusts to soak and batter them into lumps of a size it can swallow. It is also very intolerant of and quick to peck ferociously at food competitors, even when they are of quite unrelated species.

As can often be seen when it is in company with tame ducks of other species on ornamental waters, the Mallard is usually successful in competition with all other surface-feeding waterfowl of comparable or smaller size, except when the food givers deliberately use their human ingenuity in order to try to ensure 'fair shares'. The same is true when such birds as pigeons or House Sparrows compete with it on land. The Mute Swan can get the better of it, by keeping it at a distance by threat, and the Black-headed Gull sometimes manages to snatch from it large pieces of food, or bits of them as they become soaked and break off, when it is on the water.

Tufted Duck

This diving duck is only tame on some public waters. Except in the case of a few very tame individuals that will totter a few metres on land to take food from the hand or ground, the Tufted Duck can only exploit bread that is presented to it on water, either thrown in or dropped to it over bridges or the like. It is probable that the first Tufted Ducks to do so started eating bread through watching Mallards or other water-birds eating it.

The Tufted Duck is able to feed successfully on bread even in competition with Mallards or Mute Swans. It can, or at any rate does, take apparently great risks with either because of its habit of diving, with or without its booty, whenever it is threatened seriously or hemmed in by such larger birds. It is also more successful in eluding gulls than is the Mallard, because of its habit of countering the gull's lunge at the food in its bill by an immediate dive. It also 'specialises' in gleaning from the bottom or deeper water those particles of soaked bread that have been missed by the surface feeders and sunk.

The Pochard when feeding on bread, appears to use the same tactics as does the Tufted Duck. It is, however, tame in fewer places and almost always outnumbered by the Tufted Duck, which in this situation, although not when feeding on natural foods, would appear to be in direct competition with it.

Coot

The Coot is tame on many park lakes in towns, and sometimes also on suburban waters. When feeding on bread it usually does so only on or near the water and takes it with the same quick dipping pecks as when feeding on natural foods. It is not very efficient in competition with ducks or gulls but often counters its disabilities by becoming very tame and taking food directly from the hand.

I once saw a good instance of how quickly this species can learn a new food by example. During a hard winter most of Virginia Water lake was frozen, but there was one fairly extensive open area, on which were about thirty very miserable-looking Coots. I threw many pieces of bread into the water, where they slowly drifted towards the coots. Some of these ignored the bread entirely, others swam towards it, looked at and sometimes tentatively pecked it but made no attempt to eat. Obviously they had no idea that it might be edible and a cursory examination did not enlighten them. Suddenly I noticed a Coot still a little way from the bread but swimming very fast and purposefully towards it. Its eager decisive manner aroused the interest of its companions as well as my own. As soon as it reached a piece of bread it began to feed with the utmost eagerness. At once other Coots dashed towards it, snatched at the bread it was eating and also ate ravenously. Within a few moments most or all of them were also seizing bits of bread which no other Coot had hold of and within a very few moments all had been eaten. From the way in which they fed it was quite certain that they were very hungry indeed and yet they had not attempted to eat the bread, in spite of investigating it, until the experienced bird did so.

Moorhen

This bird is tame on some town and suburban waters but there are also many individuals that have learnt to eat bread on waters where the species is not tame. If pieces of bread are floated down a river or stream where one has a view to a distance they will quite often be seen to be intercepted and eaten by a Moorhen at a safe distance from the observer. It is likely that in such places the bird's usual introduction to bread has been through discarded sandwiches or bread-based baits left by anglers. Probably some of these Moorhens either tried bread as food on their own initiative, or followed the example of other species, such as House Sparrows or Black-headed Gulls.

Even in those places where it comes to man to be fed, the Moorhen is usually less ready to take food from the hand than are many other birds, and is apparently afraid to press among a crowd of other species. Under such conditions its main stratagem is to run quickly and try to snatch up any piece of bread which has landed or been dropped sufficiently far from other birds for the swift-footed Moorhen to reach and run off with it before competitors can do so.

Black-headed Gull

This is the smallest and most agile of the British gulls (leaving aside some species that only occur on passage or as stragglers) and is consequently usually the most successful in exploiting human charity in towns and suburbs, although less so when in competition with its larger congeners on garbage dumps and around harbours. Its feeding methods when taking natural foods include snatching up floating morsels and plunge-diving with (normally) only partial immersion, these two methods being used both from flight and from the water surface; taking worms and other invertebrates from the ground, either by low searching flight or by walking about holding the head in the same position as when swimming and searching; and catching winged ants and (less often) other insects in flight high in the air.

All these innate feeding patterns are made use of when feeding on bread. The Black-headed Gull seizes in flight bits of food thrown to it, or darts down to snatch them up from the water. It alights and walks about on the ground picking up food, aggressively pecking at pigeons and other birds to force them to give way to it. It takes food from high window ledges (and less often from low ones), either alighting to do so or snatching pieces as it passes in flight; and will also alight in or snatch up food from quiet streets or quite small

A man feeding Black-headed Gulls in St James' Park, London. This beautiful white and lavender grey gull with red bill and feet is abundant and widespread (by day) in London in winter. When it moults into breeding plumage it acquires the very dark coffee brown head from which it gets its name, and its bill and feet turn darker. (*RSPB, Jane Miller*)

and enclosed squares or gardens as well as from larger open spaces where it habitually feeds.

It can swallow relatively large lumps of bread very quickly and yet will pick up even very small crumbs. Again, this versatility is adapted to its natural foods which vary in size from fish about 15 cm long to tiny insects. Ducks that are trying to break up a large piece of bread on the water, are habitually harried by it and often successfully robbed. Where, as in London, the larger gulls are, with a few individual exceptions, much less tame, they get very little of the food given by man in comparison with the Black-headed, although this situation is reversed by the Herring Gull in some coastal towns where it is tame enough to crowd around humans distributing food.

Although the Black-headed Gull feeds largely on bread, it usually prefers food with a higher fat or protein content, such as fish, meat, fat, bacon rinds and cheese. These foods are often taken with extreme eagerness by individuals that are, apparently, not hungry enough to do more to bread offered them than throw it aside in disgust.

Common Gull (or Mew Gull)

In London this species finds some bread as flotsam and jetsam but most is obtained by chasing and harrying Black-headed Gulls, and to a lesser extent other birds, that are carrying a piece too large for them to swallow. It does not usually dare to attack a Black-headed Gull until the latter is at a little distance from man. Once the bread being carried is well away from humans over the river or other large expanse of water, Lesser and Greater Black-backs may join in the chase and the Common Gull, if it has succeeded in forcing the Black-headed to drop its booty, may be robbed in its turn.

Where the larger gulls are tame, the Common Gull appears to have little success in competing with them for food deliberately given by humans. It is usually present on garbage tips but, of the inland wintering gull populations as a whole, it is the species least directly dependent on man and relying most on earthworms and other natural foods.

Herring Gull

In many coastal resorts around Britain, such as Penzance, Scarborough and Lerwick, this species is quite tame, although usually quick to appreciate any signs of hostility towards it. Many individuals wait near houses or other places where they are used to being fed. They gather round anyone distributing food, seizing and swallowing large pieces and effectively eliminating the competition of other species near the point of distribution. Pieces dropped a little away

A pair of Herring Gulls and their nest. This species' preferred natural nesting places are roomy cliff ledges and recesses among rocks or cliff tops. Like some other birds with similar breeding habits it readily nests on buildings if permitted to do so (*J. B. & S. Bottomley*)

from the scrum may, however, be snatched up by a Black-headed Gull, Jackdaw, or some other more agile bird.

On garbage dumps this gull usually dominates other common species except for the Greater Black-backed Gull. More often than not a big percentage of the larger lumps of bread or other food items available on a garbage tip are eaten by it.

Feral Pigeon

As has been discussed in a previous chapter, this is a successful species in most towns, and usually the most plentiful bird in almost entirely built-up areas. In most of the older towns it probably once found its main feeding niche as a gleaner of spilled grain, but since the decline of horse traffic the places where grain can be found have become limited and localised and, in general, Feral Pigeons in large towns subsist mainly on bread.

Feral Pigeons, like other birds, soon learn to recognise the preliminary movements of a person about to give food, and also to recognise individual humans who have befriended them, even when these are showing no signs of food-giving. Otherwise the behaviour shown is the same as when feeding under natural conditions. The pigeons first alight and then search for food. They are quick to notice other pigeons feeding, or flying or running in a manner suggesting that they have found food or know where to find it.

Where they do not have to compete with crows, gulls, or Mallards, Feral Pigeons often feed to a considerable extent on large lumps of bread, in spite of the difficulty that they have in detaching pieces of suitable size. Where, however, as in many coastal towns, they have to compete with gulls and crows, these usually take any large piece of bread away from them in a matter of seconds. Here the Feral Pigeons rely on finding very small morsels which the other species have overlooked, and sometimes (where they are tamer than their competitors) on approaching benevolent humans more closely.

Some Feral Pigeons also seek food inside large stations, in moderately busy or very narrow streets and similar places where other species, except for a few individual Wood Pigeons, Jackdaws and House Sparrows, do not venture. They also often feed at night by artificial light in towns, which I have not seen Wood Pigeons or House Sparrows do, although the habit has been recorded from a few places in the latter (and other) species.

Wood Pigeon

It is highly likely that bread-eating started in this species through observation of Feral Pigeons, and possibly sometimes other birds, eating bread.

When directly competing with Feral Pigeons the Wood Pigeon is usually handicapped by a reluctance to force its way into a close crowd of birds, although some individual Wood Pigeons will do this. It has an advantage in being able to swallow larger pieces, and many Wood Pigeons habitually endeavour, often with success, to take bread out of the mouth of a Feral Pigeon that they see struggling to swallow a piece too large for it. Wood Pigeons will often persistently follow House Sparrows that have carried a piece of bread into or under cover, and although I have only seldom seen them succeed finally in seizing the bread, they may do so more often than my observations suggest.

Unlike the Feral Pigeon, which relatively seldom comes down into small London or suburban gardens, the Wood Pigeon, at least in London, quite often feeds at bird-tables or on the ground in small gardens. This increases the availability of bread to it as a species while at the same time increasing its liability to be ambushed and killed by domestic and feral cats.*

Collared Dove

This species is not (yet) established in London, although found in many parts of its periphery (July 1977). My observations on it have

---

*Shortly after I wrote the above, an adult and healthy hen Feral Pigeon that had begun to feed with the Wood Pigeons in my garden, was caught by a cat.

been in suburban or semi-rural parts of Surrey, Kent, Hertfordshire, the Scillies and the Shetlands; and Austria in and near Vienna.

In winter, at least in Britain and western Europe, and in some places in summer also, the Collared Dove relies largely or entirely on food given or spilled by man. Although it can swallow seeds as large as maize and peanuts without difficulty, its slender delicate bill is even less fitted for breaking up large lumps of bread than are those of the larger British pigeons. If the bread is fairly soft it will manage to detach pieces by the same method as the Feral Pigeon, that is by the innate tugging and shaking movements used to detach a seed from a grass ear or similar seeding part of a plant. Otherwise it relies on picking up crumbs. It will search for and eat very small crumbs of bread and other food, such as chocolate, sometimes finding them in situations where they appear to have been overlooked by House Sparrows and Feral Pigeons seeking food in the same places. However, I doubt if any crumb taken by a Collared Dove would be ignored by a hungry House Sparrow or Feral Pigeon, if seen by them; while the smallest grain likely to be fed to birds or spilled is panicum millet, which House Sparrows, Feral Pigeons and Wood

Collared Doves feeding at a bird table. This dove's rapid recent spread across Europe has been due to its ability to profit from man's activities. First seen in Britain in 1952 it is now widespread and in many places abundant. (*J. B. & S. Bottomley*)

Pigeons will all eat readily. The question of how the Collared Dove copes with competition is, therefore, of interest.

Many of its typical feeding sites – chicken runs, gardens and balconies where birds are fed, farmyards, zoos, and wildfowl collections – are free of other pigeon competitors for various reasons. Places which lack suitable nesting or roosting sites nearby, or which are more or less enclosed or overhung by trees, may not be discovered or used by Feral Pigeons, while their fear of humans in many districts has prevented Wood Pigeons from becoming tame enough to venture there; or human intolerance of the two larger species may have excluded them or limited their numbers. Either of the *Columba* species may, however, be present in any of the types of feeding sites listed above; as well as in or around the public parks, railway sidings, granaries, flour mills, and streets with cafés or food kiosks that are also habitual feeding places for Collared Doves.

Where I have seen both Collared Doves and other pigeons feeding on bread or grain supplied by man, either the supply has been superabundant or else the birds have been few (under twenty of each species) and searching for rather widely-scattered crumbs of food. This was so in Vienna in August 1966, where individual Collared Doves were seen searching the pavements and others were in parks where there was much food given and only a few Feral Pigeons, but none in the areas where large flocks of Feral Pigeons gathered to be fed. I was, however, puzzled as to why *more* Feral Pigeons did not come to some of the feeding places used by both species.

It seems surprising that the Collared Dove has managed to use the bird-table and chicken-run niches, not only in places where it is protected, and the House Sparrow is rigorously persecuted, but also in Britain where large numbers of House Sparrows, and often also of Starlings, habitually use such feeding sites. Possibly, in some cases, deliberate efforts on its behalf by bird feeders have helped the Collared Dove in gardens and at bird-tables, and its ability to find and swallow grain quickly, in chicken runs. When I have watched it feeding on bread in competition with Starlings, it has at best only managed to get odd crumbs.

Blackbird

The Blackbird takes bread very freely and may rely largely on it in winter in some cases. Its methods with pieces of bread too large to swallow are those normally used to break up large insects and to remove slime from worms.

Bread is taken most in gardens and from bird-tables, but also in public parks, around open-air restaurants, on garbage tips and in quiet streets. As has been discussed previously when dealing with the Blackbird in London, its habit of standing still for a moment before lunging forward to seize a morsel, and of pausing at intervals when breaking it up, although adaptive under natural feeding conditions, often results in loss of the bread to other species where these are competing.

The Blackbird is able to drive off most other garden passerines from food but often largely confines its aggressiveness to other typical thrushes. The Song Thrush and Redwing almost always give way to it at food (though the Song Thrush will chase it in flight) but the situation with the Fieldfare and the larger Mistle Thrush varies. Sometimes these allow themselves to be driven away by the Blackbird without any resistance but not always. In one instance a Fieldfare established itself at a bird-table in spite of the efforts of a Blackbird to drive it away, and I have seen a Blackbird apparently fear to press home an attack on a pair of Mistle Thrushes, feeding at a bird-table, when they showed no signs of giving way as it flew at them. Probably the reason that, in most observed instances, the Blackbird gets the better of these two species is because, when coming near a food source in a garden, they feel insecure in a place strange, and possibly alarming, to them, while the Blackbird is in its own territory and correspondingly confident and at ease.

The Starling seldom allows itself to be intimidated by the Blackbird. In very hard weather I have seen both Song Thrushes and Redwings take advantage of this and manage to obtain some food by feeding among a flock of Starlings in a garden, whither the resident Blackbird would not always follow them.

Robin

The Robin's acceptance of man as a food provider is almost certainly due to its innate tendency, when hungry, to approach and watch for food near any large creature that is disturbing the ground. Under natural conditions rooting pigs and other large mammals were probably the creatures most often used and man's behaviour, especially when gardening, is sufficiently similar for the bird to have easily included him. This tendency of the Robin to approach man has probably been the main factor responsible for the many commendatory legends and superstitions about it and for the sentimental affection in which it is held in Britain.

The Robin obtains bread in gardens, at bird-tables, in parks, and at picnic and open-air eating places. It uses its innate feeding methods of watching from a convenient perch and then flying down to seize a morsel, or hopping about on the ground searching. Whereas all the birds previously considered here *learn* to approach people who regularly feed them, the Robin merely has to intensify a *natural* tendency to do this and, moreover, if it is hungry, will approach them even if it has never been fed before. This, and the strong 'favouritism' usually shown towards it, enable it to be very successful where food that is actually being distributed by a human is concerned.

Dunnock

The Dunnock takes bread in gardens, on and more especially from underneath bird-tables, and in many public places where birds are fed. As with the Robin, it is usually essential that the feeding place should be within fairly short distance from cover of some kind. Although it will swallow quite large crumbs, and such large seeds as hemp and wheat, it seems to find and take great numbers of very small crumbs that have been either undiscovered or ignored by other species.

A peculiarity of the Dunnock, possibly connected with its pre-occupation with searching the ground for small morsels when seeking food, is that it does not usually appear to learn to recognise man as a food giver. I have only once ever seen a Dunnock behave as if it did so. In places such as Kew Gardens where tits, thrushes, House Sparrows, Chaffinches and Robins recognise the human food giver as such and respond positively to food thrown towards them, the behaviour of the Dunnock is in strong contrast. It often appears to understand that the gathering of other birds means a chance of food and will approach the area where the food is being given, searching the ground and picking up any morsels it can find. Any attempts to 'help' by throwing food towards it are either ignored, perhaps more likely not noticed, or they frighten the Dunnock and cause it to retreat.

Pied Wagtail

The Pied Wagtail frequently gleans crumbs along the shoreline of lakes, rivers and ponds at places where ducks or other birds are fed with bread. It then searches for and takes very small morsels that have been overlooked by larger birds. It also sometimes takes bread in similar manner in gardens, car parks, on flat roofs and other more or less open areas where birds are fed or food spilled.

During the Second World War I found that birds of the paler continental race of this species, the so-called White Wagtail, foraging around camps in the desert in Egypt and Libya, would readily take morsels of corned beef, and breadcrumbs. The Pied Wagtail usually shows fear of a piece of bread of about half its own size or more, but will sometimes, after much hesitation, attempt to pick suitable bits from a soft piece of bread of this size.

Tits

In Britain the Great Tit, the Blue Tit and the Coal Tit habitually feed at bird-tables and in gardens where birds are fed; the Marsh Tit and the Willow Tit do so less often, although regularly in some places. I have no personal observations on the Marsh Tit at bird-tables and only a few on the Willow Tit, so will confine my remarks to the first three species.

Tits at a bird-table take mainly seeds with a high oil content, such as peanuts and sunflower seeds and fat or fatty meat. They will, however, eat bread if they are hungry and there is no more favoured food available. As they take a very wide variety of natural foods which are found by active searching, it is not surprising that they should readily learn to take human foods. Apart from their agility at feeding while clinging to a lump of food hung up for them, they have none of the fear of large pieces of food shown by many species, but will fly on to them without hesitation. They will even, although often a little hesitant to come to the ground if they suspect danger, cling to a lump of bread or fat that is lying on the ground and pick pieces from it. Their ability to break up food held under their feet, and readiness to fly off with pieces as large as they can carry, also gives them some advantage.

This lack of fear of large lumps of food and their apparently instantaneous recognition of fat as food suggests that under natural conditions they may at times feed on remains of carcasses killed by large predators. So far as I know this has not been recorded but the lack of evidence may merely reflect the lack of large predators and their prey, and the plenitude of man-provided food for tits in densely-populated countries under modern conditions. On the other hand, the initial sampling of fat may be due to its having some features in common with quiescent whitish grubs such as tits must sometimes find.

It might be added that the habit of hiding surplus food is practised by Coal, Marsh and Willow Tits and may serve as some compensation for their inferior status in relation to the Great and Blue Tits, which habitually drive them from sources of human food, and sometimes rob them of food which they have hidden.

Where small birds are regularly fed and not molested the tendency of Great, Blue and Coal Tits (and on the Continent the Marsh Tit also) to become tame enough to take food from the hand, or from a closer distance than most other species will, and their deliberate solicitation of food by flying very conspicuously up to, and either perching very close or hovering in front of people, enable them to compete successfully for handouts even with Blackbirds and House Sparrows. This success is usually helped by a decided favouritism towards tits in preference to most other species, the Robin excepted.

Nuthatch

In general the behaviour of this bird, when feeding on man's bounty, closely parallels that of the tits as described above. It hides food as keenly as the Willow and Coal Tits but, unlike them, can usually drive off not only Great and Blue Tits but also Greenfinches and House Sparrows. It can carry surprisingly large pieces of food and will sometimes take bread in preference to peanuts or sunflower seeds.

Like the tits, and perhaps to a greater degree than the Great or Blue Tits, the Nuthatch usually takes bread only when it can do so without venturing more than a dozen metres or so from the nearest tree.

Starling

The Starling, although it usually prefers fat or meat in almost any form, habitually feeds on bread (and also on many farinaceous foods prepared for domestic birds and mammals) taken from bird-tables, lawns where birds are fed, rubbish tips, litter baskets, and almost all other possible sources.

The Starling is unable to hold food under foot, or to stabilise it by jamming it in a fork and it has virtually no cutting edge to its mandibles. Hence it is extremely inefficient when trying to feed from a piece of bread or fat that is too small to remain still when pecked at but too large to swallow whole. Their numbers, boldness and relative lack of intra-specific aggression ensure, however, that when Starlings are present they usually get a large proportion of the bread available.

Because it is often seen fighting over food, the Starling has an un-
justified reputation for quarrelsomeness. In fact, when feeding it usually defends, or attempts to defend, only the lump of food that it
is actually pecking at, or its position at the bird-table, pig trough,
etc. Hence many Starlings are able to feed efficiently at the same time
and place in a way which would be quite impossible for a comparable
number of Blackbirds or other thrushes.

Starlings frequently carry off pieces of bread or other food with
which they are having difficulty, presumably to get away from interference by competitors. The bird doing so usually attempts to break
up the food when it settles elsewhere; but this habit often leads to
its being robbed by larger species such as gulls and crows.

Carrion and Hooded Crow

The Crow freely takes bread and other human foods. It is common
in and around London and some other towns, as well as in all kinds
of open country. Its ability to hold objects underfoot while hammer-
ing or tearing at them, and its habit of dunking food that is difficult
to break up (especially if it is at all sticky) enable it to deal efficiently
with bread and other foods in almost any form. It habitually hides
surplus food and recovers it later.

In and near towns the Crow takes bread from large gardens, open
spaces in parks, and waste ground where birds are fed. Some individuals will approach within a few metres of man when doing so, but
even they usually flee at once if they notice that any human being
is watching them. It secures much bread in the form of crusts and
other pieces that have been dropped or left on roofs or in gutters
by Starlings and House Sparrows. It will also often pursue any bird
that it sees carrying food. On the several occasions when I have seen
a single Crow join gulls in pursuit of one of their number that was
carrying a large lump of bread, it has always succeeded in finally
getting most or all of the booty, in spite of fierce competition from
a dozen or more gulls. When I was able to see what happened, the
Crow achieved this by its ability to predict the path of the food when

it fell; when the harried gull dropped the bread, the Crow swooped accurately to intercept it. Once it had the bread it flew quickly, with only the minimum necessary dodging of attacks, into the nearest tree whither the gulls could not follow.

The Crow also habitually takes food from garbage tips. Here it usually has to compete with large gulls, and in some places also Ravens, and where this is the case it seems to obtain few large food items but to rely mainly on scavenging small morsels, especially such as are contained or hidden in paper or other wrapping.

Rook

Except as a straggler the Rook is absent from London, but it commonly forages in or around towns and suburbs that are close to its usual arable or pastoral feeding grounds. In general the remarks about the limitations imposed on the Crow by its timidity and suspicion of humans apply to the Rook, although to a lesser degree. It is more apt to come to bird-tables and smallish lawns in suburban gardens, albeit at first after much hesitation. In many towns it also forages in the early morning hours in the streets, even in some quite narrow streets, taking the remnants of the previous night's fish and chips and other food that has been flung into the gutter (see pp. 94–95).

Like the Crow it also seeks food on garbage tips and similar places. Whereas, however, many town Crows probably feed largely on bread throughout the year, it is probable that few Rooks rely on bread except in times of great scarcity of more natural foods.

Jackdaw

The Jackdaw (in Britain) frequents and feeds in towns and suburbs to a rather greater extent than either the Rook or the Crow, although in London it is virtually absent except on parts of the periphery. It is usually less afraid of man and less wary than either of the two larger species and this, and its greater agility, give it a considerable advantage over them in the acquisition of bread even though they dominate it at feeding places. Jackdaws will usually approach closer to humans than Rooks or Crows seeking bread in the same area dare to, and they will come down into relatively enclosed spaces with much less preliminary hesitation. Often while a Rook is still fearfully eyeing a piece of bread in some street or garden, a Jackdaw will dash down, seize it and bounce up and away.

In some places Jackdaws habitually visit sites where Feral Pigeons are fed and often succeed in taking any sizeable pieces of bread with which the pigeons cannot quickly deal. All three corvids readily learn to visit picnic places and other areas where people regularly eat out of doors, and to pull any papers that may possibly contain food through the sides of wire litter baskets, but the Jackdaw does so to a greater extent and usually more boldly than the Rook or Crow.

Chaffinch

The Chaffinch is the only British finch that habitually takes bread. The Greenfinch occasionally does so but usually comes to gardens and bird-tables only for seeds or grain, especially for seeds rich in oil such as peanuts, sunflower seeds or niger seed. The widespread provision of shelled peanuts by the owners of garden bird-tables has presumably been one of the factors conducing to the present position of the Greenfinch as a regular 'bird-table bird'.

The Chaffinch obtains bread from suburban and rural gardens, in parks and around open-air restaurants, snack bars, picnic sites and car parks in wooded country. In these latter places it often becomes fairly tame, occasionally sufficiently so to take food from the hand.

It appears most successful at obtaining bread where House Sparrows are few or absent; where House Sparrows are present in considerable numbers the Chaffinch usually shuffles around on the periphery, awaiting its chance to snatch up and fly off with a piece of bread, or picking up very small crumbs.

House Sparrow

The House Sparrow's original, and where possible continuing role is that of competitor or scavenger for grain grown by man or wasted in harvesting and in other ways. Over much of urban and suburban Britain, as in many places elsewhere, the House Sparrow now, however, relies very largely on bread. Anywhere around or near human habitations where bread is made available is almost certain to be visited by the House Sparrow. It is the only passerine bird, indeed the only bird except the Feral Pigeon, that habitually seeks food in fairly busy London streets, *inside* large stations, and inside some buildings.

House Sparrows usually sooner or later find any regular supply of bread that is made available, even in an area where they have not previously been seen foraging. This often happens when a feeding station is started in some park or woodland half a kilometre or so from the nearest houses. It is perhaps connected with the fact that communal roosts may be half a kilometre or more from the nearest daytime haunt of House Sparrows.

Where the House Sparrow has to compete with larger birds for limited quantities of food given by man, it is able to lay aside its usual wariness and to show trust in man. In some of the inner London parks, notably in St James's Park, House Sparrows will not merely fly up and take food from the hand but will perch calmly on the hand and feed from a piece of bread, with an apparent lack of any apprehension, such as I have not seen from any other wild small passerine when feeding from human hands.

Reed Bunting

The recent increased use of some more or less dry breeding habitats by this species and its feeding in gardens is well known. The habit of eating bread in gardens is not, however, entirely new. I first saw it in 1932 when, as a schoolboy taken by another to see his pigeons, I was astonished to see a cock Reed Bunting feeding on bread in his parents' tiny suburban garden, together with a number of House Sparrows. This was at Egham, Surrey in southern England. Reed Buntings (like Moorhens) often take bread that has been left or thrown away by anglers. It would be interesting to know whether the individuals that do this are birds that have previously learnt to eat bread in gardens in winter or whether some Reed Buntings first learn to take bread through the activities of anglers in their breeding habitats.

An example of how human attitudes affect birds' opportunities: owing to persecution our Grey Heron fears man and so is often unable to use otherwise suitable feeding areas because of his near presence. On the Galapagos Islands, the related Great Blue Heron has little fear of humans, as this photograph shows. (*Barbara Snow*)

CHAPTER SIX

FUTURE IMPERFECT

Prophesying is notoriously liable to error and, as is well known, modern scientific and economic forecasters have yet to prove themselves less fallible than their forebears. I make no claim to prediction but shall here venture to speculate on some possible future developments and the effects that they might be expected to have on the birds of man's world. Some of them are likely to have even greater effects, for good or ill, on the birds of truly wild places.

Two of the most daunting possible fates that certain gloomy prophets (not without some presumptive evidence) forecast for mankind are best dealt with first, because it seems easy to make reasonable guesses as to what their overall effects on birds would be. The first is if some worldwide catastrophe or series of catastrophes brought about the extinction of man or reduced his world status to that of a few scattered neo-primitive groups. Even if we hopefully assume that this had not been brought about by some contamination of air, earth or water that had equally harmful effects on other forms of life, it would still be disastrous for most or all of the birds we have been discussing. As first scrub and then forest reclaimed the open fields, larks, Lapwings and other open-country species would find the vast areas of habitat that man's activities had vouchsafed them being destroyed even more thoroughly and implacably than man had destroyed the original forests. Not long after those in the larger towns had starved to death the country-dwelling House Sparrows and Feral Pigeons would be finding fewer and fewer places to feed. Here and there local populations of such birds might somehow adapt to the new conditions but most, and probably all, would be doomed. Their species would indeed survive, but almost certainly only in natural habitats where they were thriving before agricultural man came on the scene.

At first those swallows and martins that nest on or in buildings might thrive as well or better than before. More ruined or half-ruined buildings to nest in, in all probability just as many insects. Depending on how long modern building materials lasted, it might be hundreds of years before these birds were forced to breed only where suitable cliffs and caves supplied natural sites, with consequent great reductions in their numbers and distribution. Birds that were originally woodland dwellers, such as tits, thrushes, the Robin and the Wood Pigeon, would fare better. Those individuals or populations among them that had come to rely on getting food, one way or another, from man, would face lean times and suffer heavy casualties but the species as a whole would be little affected. Of seabirds at least many gulls and the Fulmar would probably suffer a decrease in numbers. The Mute Swan in Britain might become largely or entirely restricted to fairly large sheets of water with extensive shallows. In former towns at least, and possibly elsewhere, the Mallard would be likely to decrease, with perhaps some consequential increases of some other waterfowl.

The situation for those birds which had not adapted well to man's works but had hung on previously only in natural or little-altered habitats would, of course, be very different. None of them would fare worse and most would fare much better for man's removal.

The situation with introduced species would, I think, be no different from those of native birds. Those dependent on the conditions created by man would be likely to die out but those which had adapted well to natural or near-natural habitats in their new countries would continue to thrive there. At least one such introduction would probably fare better. This is the Mandarin Duck in Britain. The spread of oak woods over what are now fields and other open areas, the cessation of artificial clearing of streams and ditches and the consequent increase in the areas of waterlogged woodlands, and the increase in the number of old, hole-providing trees left standing, would all result from man's demise and would all be highly favourable for the Mandarin. Any increase of natural predators would be more than offset by the removal of the sportsman and his gun and, so long as the climate did not alter drastically, this duck would continue to thrive the width of the old world away from its original home, a living memorial to some men's love of beauty.

The second very daunting hypothetical future is that, far from man being exterminated or exterminating himself, he will continue to obey the Biblical injunction (which, as a species, he has never disobeyed) to 'increase and multiply', to such an extent that his swarming multitudes and his artefacts will cover the whole earth, a few of the more inhospitably cold or hot regions possibly excluded. His food would be synthesised in laboratories or grown in soil-less cultures. I find this the more depressing of the two ideas, not because I think man would be unable to adapt to such conditions but because I think he might. In doing so he would, however, lose all those qualities that make individual men and women pleasing and human life worthwhile. Needless to say, under such conditions of intense human overcrowding the birds of man's world, like others, would go. People would almost certainly have neither the means nor the will to preserve them.

I think, however, that either of the above-discussed fates is unlikely, at least in the fairly shortish-term future. It seems more probable that man will muddle on from crisis to crisis, increasing in numbers (but not, from a global viewpoint, catastrophically so), cutting down more forests, draining more wetlands, farming more intensively and covering more land with buildings, roads and air terminals. At the same time the standard of living of most people in the so-called 'developed' countries will deteriorate and the living standards of those in so-called 'developing' countries will not significantly improve. It seems also likely that, even in democratic or nominally democratic countries, officialdom will continue to increase both the scope and severity of its control over the majority of people. How will, or rather how might these developments affect the birds of man's world?

The further spreading of the man-altered environment might be expected to cause a spreading in range of the birds we have considered in the future, as in the past. I think it is less certain, however, that this will entail an absolute increase in the numbers of such species. More intensive and more highly mechanised farming, especially when combined, are generally, in spite of the gluts of food temporarily provided, less favourable to birds than older types of husbandry. Those who farm in such a manner tend to be rather more intolerant than others of birds that seek a share of their crops, and are more likely to have the means to employ sophisticated and effective methods of killing the offending birds *en masse*.

The probable future lowering of living standards for most people in the now relatively affluent societies might not, of itself, cause any overall reduction in the number of town and village birds. After all, as we have seen, many scavenging birds thrive very well in many poor countries; casual observation in London will show that it is not the richest citizens who give most to the pigeons. However, a lowering of average living standards correlated (as it is likely to be) with an increasingly intrusive, restrictive and minatory officialdom would, I think, have a very adverse effect on all birds relying in part on human bounty. People having, and deeming themselves fit to have, authority over others are seldom at a loss to find what seem to them good and justifiable reasons for imposing restrictions on or banning the pleasures of those in their power. The possibility of transmission of diseases from birds to man (a very slight but undeniable risk), the need to save 'waste' human food (which in London in the immediate post-war years when bird-feeding was banned, was consequently burnt or thrown away), and the alleged need to keep the pavements free of bird droppings (straining at a gnat and swallowing a whole herd of camels if people and dogs are to be allowed on them) have all been cited as reasons for banning the feeding of birds or organising their destruction in the past and will, I fear, increasingly be so in the future.

As a child, the first highlight of any of my rather infrequent visits to London was feeding the pigeons in Waterloo Station. To do so there, or at any other London station, is now a crime, although the stations are certainly no cleaner than they were in my childhood.

Superstition as well as sentiment has often been of great benefit to birds living alongside man, as with the English Robin. The swallows, or at least those of them that nest in or on human dwellings, have often been protected as birds of good omen, and in Tibet it was formerly accounted a very lucky thing to have a pair of Choughs nest in one's house. In other countries religion (I do not propose here to venture to discuss the vexed question of where religion ends and superstition begins or vice-versa), notably Buddhism, has sometimes led to a non-violent and in effect protective attitude towards wild birds even though it has seldom saved domestic animals from gross ill-treatment. Much of Tibet, and especially the holy city of Lhasa and its environs, was virtually a wild bird sanctuary, so far as freedom from human persecution was concerned. It would probably be depressing for bird-lovers to know what the situation in Tibet is now under Chinese Communist rule.

Judging by the campaigns against the Tree Sparrow that have been organised in China itself, it is unlikely that their new masters will have looked kindly on the Tibetans' toleration of grain-eating species. Such previously abundant large and edible birds as the Eastern Rock Pigeon and Bar-headed Goose may well have been exploited for food. If, as is likely, the Buddhist creed has been partly or largely discredited by their Chinese rulers it is quite possible that the Tibetans' attitudes and actions towards their birds may have altered to the latter's disadvantage. It would be interesting to know just what changes have taken place since the pre-war years, when at least one German and one British ornithologist spent (separately) much time in Tibet. It seems unlikely that anyone from the western democracies will be allowed to visit and freely observe either birds or humans in Tibetan towns either now or in the near future.

I think, however, that there are at least two cheering factors (for those who are cheered at the thought of birds continuing to share man's world) that may, and I hope will, offset the baleful effects of increased control by officials. First it may well be that, as seems to have happened very widely in the past sixty years or so, aesthetic and compassionate appreciation of birds will spread, gaining hold in more cultures where it was absent or vestigial before. Second, officials, and those people powerful enough to carry weight with them, although often much concerned about rare birds in wild and beautiful places, are now generally indifferent or even hostile to the 'common' species, but this attitude might change. Even if, as I hope, there will long remain *some* wild places inhabited by their appropriate birds, decreasing living standards, the likely exhaustion of fossil fuels, and the probable consequent increase of international suspicion if not outright hostility, might make it less and less possible for even 'important' people to enjoy them. Those of them who were 'hooked' on birds would then have to turn to the common birds around them (I hopefully assume there still would be such) and, perhaps, seeing at last with fresh vision the fiery eye and rainbow neck of the Feral Pigeon on the station or the vermilion bill and legs of the snow-white and pearl-grey Black-headed Gull just outside it, would be less unsympathetic towards people who delight in such creatures. Perhaps, I like to think, those who are young when they read this book may live to see an official notice on Waterloo Station that reads: 'Please feed the Pigeons'!

SCIENTIFIC NAMES OF BIRDS DISCUSSED IN TEXT

178 *Scientific names of birds discussed in text*